COPING WITH CARING

Daily Reflections for Alzheimer's Caregivers

by

LYN ROCHE

ELDER BOOKS
Forest Knolls, California

A portion of the proceeds from the sale of this book
will be donated to Alzheimer's research, in the
memory of Gene Robinson and in the hope a
prevention is soon found.

Library of Congress Cataloging in Publication Data
Main Entry Under Title:
Coping With Caring: Daily Reflections for Alzheimer's
Caregivers
Roche, Lyn
1. Alzheimer's disease 2. Dementia 3. Caregiving
4. Devotional calendars

LCCN 96-083441
ISBN O-943873-29-0

Printed in the United States of America

Cover Design: Bonnie Fisk-Hayden

Dedication

This book is lovingly dedicated to my husband, my teacher, and my editor — Bill Roche. Without his unwavering support and encouragement, my writing and this book would not have been possible.

Acknowledgments

I especially want to thank my mother, Jane Robinson, and my father-in-law, Bill Roche, Sr., both of whose devoted years of caregiving were the inspiration for *Coping with Caring*.

I am grateful to the leaders, caregivers and friends who make up the Alzheimer's Support Network in Naples, Florida. The sharing over the years of experiences, knowledge, resources, and tips richly contributed to the making of this book.

A big thanks to all the wonderful caregivers who took the time to answer my questionnaires.

My sincere appreciation to Carmel Sheridan, the founder and director of Elder Books, for sharing my belief in the need for a supportive non-technical book of this kind for family caregivers.

I am eternally thankful to God for his presence and gentle nudging every step along the way.

L.R.

Foreword

Family caregivers know what Alzheimer's disease and related disorders mean. They don't need any technical mumbo-jumbo or medical rhetoric to understand the impact of AD on their lives. From the first brush with denial, it is clear life as they know it will never be the same.

Coping with Caring: Daily Reflections for Alzheimer's Caregivers addresses the simple daily necessities of survival. An emotionally and physically healthy caregiver is essential. As the title suggests, each day must be taken one at a time. Sometimes the busy caregiver can't find a moment of solitude to reflect upon the present moment as it relates to their affected loved one. Rarely is there time for reading a lengthy article addressing the patient's condition. *Coping with Caring* meets these challenges with simple reflections offering encouragement and practical caregiving tips. One doesn't need to be a speed reader to benefit quickly from the guidance offered here.

We are all on a spiritual journey. At times we face the loneliness and isolation brought about by confronting a formidable foe. AD doesn't

mean the end of the caregiver's life. Caregiving
can be a rewarding experience. Caregivers often
come through the experience vastly enriched.
Coping with Caring offers consistent daily
support laced with loving humor, compassion and
tips grounded in reality.

Bill Roche, editor
Naples, Florida

Introduction

Coping with Caring is written for you, the family caregiver who cares for a loved one with Alzheimer's disease (AD) or a related disorder at home. The book addresses the effects of progressive dementia from the initial stages through moderately severe stages. Your loved one may be a spouse, a parent, or any other family member. *Coping with Caring* sometimes refers to the loved one as being male, sometimes female. Each page in the book provides a daily reflection from the caregiver's viewpoint followed by a practical tip for the day. The book can be used as a mini-support group meeting anytime you need it. Refer to the handy index to find immediate help with the concerns, feelings, and challenges you encounter. Don't limit the book to just one year of use. You'll be surprised how it will continue to help as you experience changes in the disease and in your caregiving role.

Sharing from caregiver to caregiver is valuable. The tips presented here are just a sampling. Use the space at the bottom of each page to add your own thoughts and solutions to the challenges you meet. Pass them on. They are meant to be shared!

If you don't presently belong to a family caregiver support group, I strongly urge you to consider joining one. If there isn't one in your area call the Alzheimer's Association national headquarters at 1-800-272-3900.

You are not alone on your journey.

Lyn Roche
Naples, Florida

JANUARY

JANUARY 1

I feel good knowing I am a caregiver, not a caretaker. I give care lovingly and freely. I don't take away from my loved one. I won't do for him something he can still do for himself. That would be taking, not giving. It is my aim to respect his dignity at all times. I offer support sometimes with just a smile — sometimes with a hand — always with love.

Today's Tip: In the early stages do as much as you can together. Take the trips. Visit family and friends. Attend reunions.

JANUARY 2

The beginning stages of Alzheimer's disease (AD) may be depressing to my loved one. The realization that something is wrong can be devastating and frightening. I will do everything I can to reassure him and show him unconditional love. He needs to know I am here for him, now maybe more than ever before.

Today's Tip: Caregivers often ask if their loved one should be told they have Alzheimer's. There are no absolutes. It may depend on how early it is diagnosed and on your individual circumstances. Do what is comfortable for you. If your loved one asks what is wrong with him, you may wish to merely say, "You have a memory problem."

JANUARY 3

My loved one and I both have feelings and emotions. We may not communicate them in the same ways anymore, but they are there. Today I will be careful and sensitive to her spirit as well as my own. I will be aware of ways to reaffirm her value. A smile on my face can do a lot for both of us.

Today's Tip: A hug is the best form of communication. Also a massage or back rub can be very satisfying to your loved one. A pleasing voice and a gentle touch will go a long way in helping her feel secure and safe. Remember skin sensitivity changes with dementia, so don't hug too tightly and make sure your touch is always soft and loving.

JANUARY 4

The Alzheimer's support group in my community provides the outside help my loved one and I need. Through its literature, support group meetings, assistance in locating local resources, and all its many other services, I have found caring and knowledgeable help. When faced with the many challenges this disease brings, I am thankful for an organization that truly understands my needs. I know I am powerless over the disease. I do, however, have control over the ways I deal with it. I will continue to make use of all the tools available to me.

Today's Tip: If you cannot find an Alzheimer's Support Group in your community, call the National Alzheimer's Association's toll free number 800-272-3900. They can provide you with literature and direct you to the chapter nearest you. It may be the most important phone call you'll ever make.

JANUARY 5

Right now I am the most important person in my loved one's life. I will do everything I can to stay strong and healthy. I will particularly watch my stress level and try to keep stress to a minimum. I need to eat good food, exercise, and get rest. I will make time for myself and my well-being. I'm doing this for my loved one and for myself.

Today's Tip: Loss of independence is hard for anyone. Your loved one is gradually losing some of his. You may be feeling you are, too. Even though at times it might not seem like it, you still have control over yours. You may find yourself having to restructure certain aspects of your life, but make sure you maintain some interests and activities of your own.

JANUARY 6

We can all get out of sorts and nasty if things don't go our way. I'll work at creating a loving environment for my loved one and myself today. I'll not be anxious about anything. Whatever gets done today is enough. What is really important is my loved one's and my serenity. I realize they can go hand in hand. If I offer her peace and tenderness, I will find peace also.

Today's Tip: If it is possible in the very early stages of AD, involve your loved one in making decisions about her future. This will help relieve you of feelings of total responsibility and guilt.

JANUARY 7

I take pride in caregiving. It is not a role I would have chosen, but it has forced me to accomplishments I would not otherwise have achieved. I applaud the courage it takes daily and it's okay to pat myself on the back. I am growing and learning new tools to help me as challenges arise. I'm doing a good job!

Today's Tip: Dementia decreases the ability to comprehend what an object is used for. Words alone don't always make sense. It helps to see things. Showing someone an action is often more effective than words. It may help to quietly model what you do with an object. Your loved one will be grateful to watch you so he can copy you. This can be most helpful at mealtime.

JANUARY 8

God is love. He doesn't cause the heartache in our lives. If we let him he can bring good out of difficult times. By letting love in every day I know he is here with me and my loved one, helping us. We are not alone. God's love comes in many forms throughout the day — in the kind voice of a friend on the phone, a bright cardinal in the yard, a smiling face at the grocery store, and in the trusting hand of my loved one held warmly in mine.

Today's Tip: The days and weeks of adjusting to the diagnosis of AD and the changes it will bring can be a special time of sharing and talking while communication is still at a fairly normal level. You may wish to express some gratitudes you've never actually spoken out loud before. Although love is expressed in many ways, it feels good to know we have told our loved ones how important they are to us.

JANUARY 9

     Friends and family members often want to help out, but they don't really know how. I need to reach out to them for my sake and for theirs. Primary caregivers can get burned out. I also realize that care responsibilities increase with time. When sincere people offer help, I can discuss the areas they feel comfortable with. I must also be honest and specific in identifying areas where I need help.

Today's Tip: Keep a list of people to call on for help. Make a record of the help you accepted and note the results. Provide literature about Alzheimer's to those who help out so that they are familiar with what you are experiencing. This caring network will help you and your loved one stay close to family and friends.

JANUARY 10

Sometimes I take life and myself so seriously I forget about having a sense of humor. Starting today I will allow joy and laughter in. Difficult situations can be refreshed with lightness. A good laugh can relieve stress and tension while putting troublesome situations in the right perspective. Along with this awareness and the lifting of my spirits I will be willing to play and take a break more often. My loved one's stress and anxiety levels are influenced by mine. We'll both benefit from some good hearted chuckles and comic relief sprinkled throughout our days.

Today's Tip: Old pictures of the important people in your loved one's life may be more recognizable to her than recent photos. Try displaying the older pictures. They should be calming and reassuring for her. If you display more recent pictures, she may repeatedly ask, "Who is this?" as she struggles to identify the people in them.

JANUARY 11

I often find myself in difficult situations I can't control. I do have control over my attitude and how I personally deal with the situations. I can do something today that will nurture my mind, body and spirit. My attitude is sure to improve if I nurture all three. For starters; I might read a good book, take a refreshing walk with my loved one, and spend some time in meditation. Healthy activities will help me dwell on positives rather than negatives. My attitude is a powerful thing.

Today's Tip: If you find there are a lot of things you want to get done this week, write them down in order of priority. Do priority one first — at your loved one's pace — then two, three, etc. If everything doesn't get done by the end of the week — so what? At least the priorities at the top of your list will probably get done and anxiety levels can be kept at a minimum for all concerned.

JANUARY 12

I have a need for fellowship and so does my loved one. I will take advantage of the adult day care facilities in my community. I can use this time to maintain my friendships and interests. It's natural for us to need a break from each other. Some separation is healthy and required to avoid over-dependence. We can both come together refreshed after a day spent with others.

Today's Tip: If your loved one doesn't always put things away, don't assume he has gotten lazy. He may need some items left out where he can see them. He can't always remember where they are if you put them away, causing him embarrassment, frustration, and further loss of independence. For now, peace for both of you may come in the form of mild clutter!

JANUARY 13

Some of the solutions I try just don't work! I need to remember there are no rights or wrongs. What works one day may not another day. What works for someone else's relative won't always work for mine. I know I am doing the best I can.

Today's Tip: Your loved one may need help with bathing. Tub baths can be difficult and dangerous. Shower water on top of her head might frighten her. Hand-held shower nozzles, rubber non-slip strips on the shower floor, and sturdy, well placed grab bars help to ease an often precarious task.

JANUARY 14

Today is a new challenge. I don't look back. Focusing on what used to be is not productive. I choose to look only at today. I won't rush through it. Helping my loved one have a good day gives me pleasure. I'll also take time to do something nice for myself today. Perhaps I'll buy a pretty plant, work on a favorite hobby, or call an old friend.

Today's Tip: Keep a package of refrigerator cookies handy as a fun diversion when your loved one gets restless or difficult. Just slice and bake a few. Your loved one may even like to help. In just minutes you can enjoy warm cookies together. The delicious smell of cookies baking is comforting and soothing for everyone!

JANUARY 15

Sometimes I think no one could possibly understand what I'm going through. Those times are exactly when I need to confide in and share with a close friend. If I isolate myself I will only enclose myself in loneliness. That would not be good for my loved one or me. I will reach out to someone else today. Through that fellowship I may see things in a different light.

Today's Tip: Giving up driving can be one of the most difficult issues for your loved one to face. Driving was one of our first signs of real independence. No wonder we fight giving it up! If he is so resistant that nothing seems to work, try removing his car from the premises for awhile. Seeing his car and being told he cannot drive it can cause a lot of anxiety.

JANUARY 16

I realize I do better when I deal with just one day at a time. Today is a new day. I will focus on it and enjoy the ever-present now. There is much in this day I can take pleasure in if I allow myself. By not dwelling on tomorrow or obsessing over yesterday I will be open to see just how precious today is!

Today's Tip: Without realizing it, your loved one may develop a grip that is uncomfortable for you. She has no control over the amount of strength she exerts. When she clutches your hand or arm too tightly, try putting a tennis ball or small stuffed animal in her hand.

JANUARY 17

Real love doesn't keep score. It is unconditional. Not only do I need to remember this in terms of my love for others, I need to apply the same kind of love to myself. The unconditional love I give to others and to myself is very freeing. We are all God's beloved children.

Today's Tip: Your loved one's body temperature can be affected by AD. He may change the thermostat often. He might close all the air conditioning vents. He may go through a period of wearing many layers of clothing which could be the result of feeling cold or from confusion. If his brain tells him he is cold, he will feel cold even though you may be feeling warm under the same conditions.

JANUARY 18

Life is full of changes. Some we expect. Some we don't. The people in our lives change. Right now my life is filled with changes I didn't expect and don't want. I can't control them. Neither can my loved one. What I can control is the way I face these changes. I will love myself and my loved one through the changes.

Today's Tip: If there is a job your loved one enjoys doing like making beds or setting the table, let her do it. Keeping busy and active is good. Tasks should not be taken away just because they aren't done the way they used to or at the speed they used to. Helping can be a very rewarding and calming activity for her as long as it is at her pace. While she is occupied with a task, you'll have time to do other things.

JANUARY 19

I may not always get the support and understanding from my family I would like. They might be in denial. I may have been there myself. I am told it is a normal stage we go through. I am fortunate to receive information, support and understanding through reaching out to others who have experienced many of the things I am now experiencing. I know I am making the best decisions and choices with the information available to me.

Today's Tip: Your local Alzheimer's Association chapter should have a larger and more up-to-date library on AD than your public library. The people there are also valuable sources of information. Generally their books are available on a borrow and return at your convenience basis. Take advantage of their services and stay informed on current research as well as helpful and new information regarding caregiving.

JANUARY 20

Today is a special gift from God. There is
wonder and awe in the awakening of a new day.
I will sharpen my awareness of how much there is
to enjoy even in the ordinariness of my day. I'll
try not to take things for granted and be thankful
for blessings large and small. I also know that
God can be counting on me to be a blessing to
someone today.

Today's Tip: People with dementia can't be
rushed or pushed. This may take extra patience
and planning on your part. Allow a little more
time to get to appointments or to accomplish a
joint task so you don't experience anxiety and
frustration. Be good to yourself and take it easy.

JANUARY 21

I am thankful for my inner strength. I have the ability to accomplish many things and find the solutions to many problems. I trust the common sense God has given me. I know when something is too much for me to handle alone. This inner strength keeps me strong and yet protects me from overdoing.

Today's Tip: Trying to reason with your loved one can be upsetting and exhausting for both of you. If he insists something is true that you know is not true, try discussing something else. Or you might get good results by just agreeing with him for a moment — then move on to another subject or a pleasant activity.

JANUARY 22

When my attitude and expectations are rigid, I put up a barrier that stops the natural flow of love. I don't want to do that. I need all the love I can get and so does everyone I come in contact with today! Unreal expectations confine and imprison us in frustration. Love and acceptance are freeing.

Today's Tip: If your loved one resists your efforts to get him to day care, try using a van service. Many day care facilities provide one. You might find that he'll go in the van eagerly because he likes riding with his day care friends. He may also respond well to the driver and get on the bus willingly.

Denial sometimes plays a big part in our thinking. Denial can keep me from accepting certain things have changed and will continue to change. This is especially true when it pertains to things I would not have chosen and have no control over. I must come out of denial to acquire the tools I need to face the challenges and realities of change.

Today's Tip: Many caregivers find other family members and friends remain in denial long after the caregiver has gone through this initial stage. The caregiver has moved on to acceptance and reality; partly because of the responsibilities and the day-to-day contact with their loved one. Preserved social skills on the part of your loved one can fool people who only see her occasionally.

JANUARY 24

I realize my loved one may no longer be able to respond to my feelings in a rational way. It helps when I can discuss my frustrations and feelings with others who care and understand. They may be old friends, family, clergy, counselor, or fellow caregivers. I need to seek out listening ears that accept me and with whom I can be truthful. Isolation can turn to depression. I will reach out and share with someone today.

Today's Tip: Sharing feelings with a trusted friend can be therapeutic. Sharing helps us step back and see things in a better perspective. Sometimes we uncover humor as we relate a difficult event or behavior. We might actually find ourselves laughing!

JANUARY 25

When I look for value and good in others I also find it in myself. When I choose to see the positives in a situation, I see myself in a more positive light. When I am patient with others, I can be more patient with myself. When I see others through loving eyes, I can love myself more readily. We are, after all, fellow travelers and mysteriously connected on our individual journeys through life.

Today's Tip: Male caregivers find themselves having to do shopping they never did before. Often a sister or close female friend can help organize this activity, especially in the beginning. Buying their loved one's personal items and clothing is one area of shopping many men never feel comfortable with. They frequently ask their loved one's sister, daughter, or best friend to do this shopping.

JANUARY 26

Swimming against the stream is futile and exhausting. When I flow with the tide, I am usually better off. I am learning I cannot struggle with my loved one over some issue without upsetting both of us. If it is not an issue of safety perhaps I need to stop and decide what is important in the long run. What really matters after all? If it is an issue of safety, I need to determine an effective way of handling it.

Today's Tip: Sometimes it is better if a cooperative authority figure (i.e. doctor, judge, policeman) tells your loved one he cannot drive any longer. This often makes a stronger impact. It also takes the blame off you. You can always say, "The doctor (judge, policeman) said you can't drive right now." It may help to then show him the written doctor order (court ruling, or ticket). Follow this by quickly changing the subject or suggesting a pleasant activity.

JANUARY 27

I have responsibilities to myself. If they are not met I cannot help anyone else. I can assist another person if I don't lose myself in the process. When another person's dependence on me begins to affect my emotional and physical health I need to take a break, seek help with the caregiving, and pursue some of my own interests. I need to do whatever it takes to get back in touch with my healthy self. I must be good to myself to be of any value to another.

Today's Tip: Many community services offer respite care. Check your AD support group, churches, and government agencies. Often they will come to your home. Some assisted living, secure care or skilled care facilities offer short-term respite on a per day charge in their facility.

JANUARY 28

Some days I just don't have any time for myself! Caregiving together with household chores puts many demands on me. I need to take a little time for me and my space. Today I will make time to enjoy a favorite magazine or a good book, or maybe just sit — whatever I need for my peace. The laundry or vacuuming can wait!

Today's Tip: A memory-impaired person may try to remember things by writing lists. They may also find safe places for things they are afraid of losing or forgetting. You might think they are hiding them or have lost them. They are most likely trying to hold on to them.

JANUARY 29

Success is measured in many different ways. I don't have to be famous or wealthy in monetary terms to be successful. I measure my success by the quality of my personal relationships. I'd rather be rich in spirit and a value to my loved ones than a famous millionaire.

Today's Tip: Your loved one's television habits or preferences may change. She might have trouble following a story. She may project herself into the story. Children's programs could become her favorites or she may enjoy programs that feature nostalgic music.

JANUARY 30

I am learning to smell the roses. Out of necessity I take things at a slower pace lately. Small things bring me pleasures I might not have noticed before. I appreciate the courtesies and kindness of others. I may not be getting all the things done I want to or at the pace I would like. That's okay. What I am doing is very important!

Today's Tip: If you are a female caregiver and you aren't mechanical, don't waste your time and energy on fix-it projects you never did before. Ask a male relative, neighbor or friend to help with those tasks. If you don't have someone close, check your telephone book for a handyman. You might find a volunteer through your church.

JANUARY 31

I am grateful for the gift of a new day. I will treat it and everyone I encounter today with respect, including myself. I will nurture my spirit with something meaningful to me. I can choose to enjoy beautiful music, good literature, or some quiet time.

Today's Tip: Listening to music can be one of the most soothing and calming activities for your loved one. It doesn't demand anything. Playing favorite music could provide meaningful quiet time for both of you.

FEBRUARY

FEBRUARY 1

Keeping things simple makes my life easier and more manageable. Knowing what really matters in life has removed unnecessary pressures. I am more content and peaceful. This allows those around me to be more content. I have let go of unreal expectations regarding myself and others. I see things in a much better light.

Today's Tip: Remember to speak to your loved one calmly. Slowing down your speech and actions will greatly help your communication with him. Don't forget eye contact is very important!

FEBRUARY 2

I choose to start each day with faith. Faith replaces fear. Faith gives me strength to do whatever is necessary today and every day. I am never alone. My faith gives me inner strength and peace.

Today's Tip: Try not to approach your loved one suddenly or from behind. Being approached unexpectedly can frighten her causing unnecessary agitation.

FEBRUARY 3

I don't compare myself to others. No situation is exactly like mine. I learn and grow from sharing with others, but we each have some special factors that affect our individual circumstances. These particular differences need to be respected. I consider all the information I have. Then I do what I believe is best for my loved one and for me.

Today's Tip: If your loved one goes through a modest stage and does not want to be totally undressed even in front of you, be creative. You can have her slip straps attached with Velcro or buttons that can be undone easily. The slip can be pulled down once her nightshirt is on. Also you can give her showers in a slip if she is more comfortable that way. The wet slip can be removed easily as you help her dry and dress.

FEBRUARY 4

All of life's experiences are valuable. I may not be aware at the time, but experiences and how I deal with them make me who I am. I am molded by both the painful and the joyful happenings in my life.

Today's Tip: Fatigue usually brings out the worst in us. Whatever areas we are weak in seem to manifest themselves when we are overtired. If you aren't getting enough rest, try to find a way to insure that you do. If your loved one is not sleeping well at night, talk to his doctor. Mild medication carefully prescribed by his physician, or more daytime activity for your loved one may be in order.

FEBRUARY 5

I meet challenges with strength, wisdom and love. All of life has purpose. I'm not stumped by what life offers. I do the best I can with what I have. I prefer to dwell on positives and I look for meaning in all I encounter.

Today's Tip: Be aware that your loved one is constantly changing. Something that works well for you now may not work six months from now. Your creativity in discovering solutions is increasing. You'll find yourself meeting new challenges fairly easily. Also, a difficult stage your loved one is in now may pass quickly.

FEBRUARY 6

Everyone needs love. When I respond to another's need for love I often discover an inner peace I hadn't expected. Freely giving love and care to someone else can show God's love for them. I may be the only instrument God is using right now to show that love.

Today's Tip: Your loved one's ability to judge temperatures can be lost early on. Monitor the use of hot water faucets and anything else that could cause burns. It's a good idea to turn down the temperature on your hot water heater.

FEBRUARY 7

Praise is important to all of us. I'll remember to praise my loved one's abilities, actions and choices today. I will accompany my words of praise with smiles and gentle pats on the back. I am aware that I need praise for my abilities, actions and choices today, too. I'll pat myself on the back if no one else does!

Today's Tip: It's best not to ask your loved one if she remembers something. It can be frustrating and depressing for her. Also don't ask fill-in-the-blank questions. If you find family or friends doing this, take them quietly aside and ask them not to.

FEBRUARY 8

It may not be within my power to change some things, but it is in my power to make choices. Sometimes I find my choices are between the lesser of two evils. I have the power of choice nevertheless. I will not see myself as a victim. I am free to make decisions and choices.

Today's Tip: Outings with your loved one should be stress-free for both of you. Take him to non-threatening places. Try to get out often. It can prevent both of you from feeling isolated.

FEBRUARY 9

Life sometimes brings the unexpected. The longer I live and the more I grow, I realize what matters is the ease with which I accept what life offers. How I face life's challenges can be more important than the challenges themselves. They need not be obstacles to my peace and growth. They often open up new understanding and insights I would not otherwise have.

Today's Tip: Clothing that goes over your loved one's head may become a source of fear and agitation for her. Clothes with full front openings are better. If she cannot dress herself but is constantly undoing front openings, try clothing with zippers or buttons on the back.

FEBRUARY 10

I used to think that *cope* was a passive word. I have learned otherwise. Coping has nothing to do with tolerating. *Cope* is a positive word and it rhymes with hope! The definition of *cope* is to manage successfully. I am a great manager!

Today's Tip: A frown on your face might make your loved one feel he has done something wrong. A smile is reassuring and sends a message of loving acceptance.

FEBRUARY 11

Nutritious meals are of major importance to all of us. The atmosphere in which they are offered is equally important. I take care to present our meals in a loving manner and in a peaceful setting. I also realize that rushing through mealtime is not good for anyone's digestion or disposition.

Today's Tip: Soft background music can be beneficial at mealtime. Instrumental music is usually the best. Remember, we all are social and no one likes to eat alone.

FEBRUARY 12

Reality is truth. The more in touch I am with reality, the better equipped I am to deal with it. I am not afraid of truth. I equip myself with as much knowledge and truth as I can. It is not an unknown or scary thing. It is simply reality.

Today's Tip: Creating a memory collage with your loved one may be fun and helps to stimulate conversation. Make the collage from old meaningful pictures of family, past trips, and past homes. The use of children's blunt scissors and a glue stick help to make the project safer and easier.

FEBRUARY 13

True values in life are sometimes uncovered in ways I would never have imagined. I've always heard simple pleasures in life were the best. Somehow I never understood the full meaning until now. Lately I see all the unexpected ways of showing, giving, and accepting love. It is clear and childlike in its simplicity.

Today's Tip: Sorting is a skill that seems to be retained for a long time. Your loved one may enjoy doing chores that involve sorting such as helping with the laundry or setting the table.

FEBRUARY 14

Life is full of new information and truths causing continuous revisions on my part. Just when I think I know it all, something changes! I am learning to stay informed and flexible. I certainly don't get bored!

Today's Tip: Your loved one may not appear to comprehend some things that are said to her. This does not necessarily mean she doesn't understand anything. Make sure no one talks about her as if she isn't in the room. Her feelings and dignity should be protected at all times.

FEBRUARY 15

The wiser I am, the more effective I become. I stay alert to the world around me and to myself. The more I understand my strengths and my limitations, the more able I am to deal with the world around me. I am growing in wisdom. I make sound judgments based on what the world has to offer and how well I truly know myself.

Today's Tip: The presence of a gentle pet usually has a positive influence on people. Petting and talking to a dog or cat can be soothing to your loved one. If you don't have a pet, a realistic stuffed animal may work well. Alternatively, occasional visits with a relative's or a neighbor's pet can be arranged.

FEBRUARY 16

Balance plays an important part in my life. It keeps me healthy — physically and emotionally. Balance is a blend of knowing I can be there for someone else and for myself at the same time. It's knowing what I can do and what I can't do. It is a mixture of doing what needs to be done along with doing what I like to do. Balance helps keep my life in proper perspective.

Today's Tip: A daily outdoor walking routine is excellent exercise. When the weather is not conducive you might find a walk through your favorite indoor shopping mall is the answer. After walking, window shopping can be a pleasant activity.

FEBRUARY 17

Today I give myself permission to bask in some personal joy. It's okay to kick up my heels and enjoy something I've been missing! If today is not convenient I will make arrangements for a special day for me tomorrow. It might be a luncheon and shopping adventure with a close friend, a sports activity like bowling or golfing, or any way I choose to pamper myself. I'm worth it! I deserve it!

Today's Tip: If your loved one does not read any longer or his eyesight prohibits reading the books he once enjoyed, you may find reading out loud to him is relaxing and enjoyable for both of you.

FEBRUARY 18

Human beings need to reach out to one another. This is a powerful fact of life. My loved one reaches out to me. I reach out to family, friends, other caregivers — wherever I find needed strength. It is a beautiful way to refresh ourselves and others. We are not meant to be solitary creatures.

Today's Tip: Some caregivers find showering their loved ones easier if they get in the shower with them.

FEBRUARY 19

By letting go of the past and not obsessing about the future, I am able to fully experience today. I can feel my feelings while they are happening. I can sort out the pains and joys of today -- today! When I experience both pain and joy as they come, I am more true to myself and those around me.

Today's Tip: For the most part television is a passive activity. Too much of it is not good for anyone, but you may find a particular program has a calming influence on your loved one. A taped copy of the program might come in handy sometime.

FEBRUARY 20

I have a choice about where I focus my attention. I can choose to dwell on the negatives or on the positives in any given situation. The choice is mine. I find the more I choose to dwell on the positives the more it becomes a habit to do so. As this comes more naturally, I experience serenity.

Today's Tips: If your loved one tends to put small objects into her mouth or she can't distinguish between what is edible and what is not, be sure to tell day care workers or anyone else she may be with.

FEBRUARY 21

I will let those I love be perfectly themselves. None of us is perfect, but we are each perfectly individual. I won't be hard on anyone, including myself. I will not put my expectations of anyone into a confining box. I am open to the wonder of all of us!

Today's Tip: Asking your loved one for her help is important. We all need to feel valuable. Be attentive to her abilities. Look for things she does well and can feel good about doing for you. Show appreciation for her help.

FEBRUARY 22

I rejoice in differences! No two entities are made exactly alike. Every snowflake is unique. No two people are identically created, not even twins. I respect and marvel at everyone's singular individuality — my own included. We are all originals!

Today's Tip: Liquid soap on a large sponge works better in the shower than bar soap. Also having all items handy and ready before the shower helps a lot. Advance preparation can go a long way in easing the situation for all concerned.

FEBRUARY 23

At times I feel drained. I need to stop and determine if I am trying to do too much. Is there any time for myself? Am I getting enough rest? These are important questions I can't afford to ignore. I'm only human. Exhaustion on my part won't help anyone. I must be honest with myself. My own health is as important as my relative's.

Today's Tip: Many care facilities offer short-term overnight respite. Your loved one can visit for a few days while you get the rest you need or a well deserved vacation! If this is not available in your area, ask a close family member or friend for help.

FEBRUARY 24

The bond I share with other caregivers is a beautiful gift. We not only care for our loved ones, we truly care for each other. We understand one another as perhaps no one else can. I'm thankful for the sustaining friendships I've made through my support group.

Today's Tip: Some AD loved ones become sensitive to sounds. The noise of the vacuum cleaner, electric mixer, and many other familiar sounds might cause agitation.

FEBRUARY 25

Reacting on impulse can get me into trouble. I hurt myself and others when I don't practice self-control. If I exercise patience and tolerance we're all better off. When faced with a situation I want to scream about, I'm learning to ask myself, "How important will this be tomorrow?" This usually works. When it doesn't, I go somewhere alone where I can't be heard — like the bathroom. I close the door and scream!

Today's Tip: You may feel more comfortable if in-home-care helpers visit a few times when you are at home before they stay alone with your loved one.

FEBRUARY 26

Most crises shrink to a workable size if I calmly collect the facts and then sort out my options. I make better decisions when I take time to do this. Sometimes discussing the situation with a knowledgeable caring person who is not involved can help too.

Today's Tip: Weight loss in AD patients is not uncommon, but every significant weight loss should be checked out with a physician to rule out other causes. If you think your loved one is not getting enough food, ask the doctor about food supplements. There are canned dietary supplements available. You can make great milk shakes by adding ice cream to them.

FEBRUARY 27

When I treat people the way I want to be treated everything seems to go better. Kindness breeds kindness. Today I will give everyone I encounter the same consideration I would expect them to give me. Everyone's day will be brighter.

Today's Tip: Assistance with insurance forms and claims can help eliminate caregiver stress. If you don't have a relative or close friend who can give you a helping hand in this area, check with your church office or your local council on aging. Many times people volunteer to do this.

FEBRUARY 28

I try never to postpone good times. Today is all I have. Yesterday is gone and tomorrow is not certain. If there is a chance to experience some joy today, I'll participate. I always find joy whenever I open my eyes and my heart to it. I'm looking out for joy today!

Today's Tip: When someone comes to visit and your loved one doesn't recognize who they are, you might want to cue your loved one. This can be done without embarrassing anyone. For instance, you could help by saying, "Here comes our neighbor Bob."

MARCH

MARCH 1

Prayer is a part of my everyday life. I offer up praise and prayers of thankfulness for my many blessings. I pray for the well-being of others. I ask God for personal strength and understanding. I am never alone when I practice God's presence through my prayer life.

Today's Tip: Don't be on the defensive if your loved one accuses you of stealing or hiding something of his. Life will run smoother for both of you if you just offer to help find his missing belongings. Even if you can't find the items, your concern and helpfulness will be appreciated.

MARCH 2

I am responsible for my own happiness. No one else can make me happy. It's not anyone else's job. I am as happy as I choose to be. The way I see the world and my individual happiness is entirely my choosing.

Today's Tip: If your loved one has to be with you constantly and is right behind you every time you turn around, you are experiencing shadowing. It is a condition that will pass, but can be unnerving. Some caregivers have found relief by writing a note which explains why they are out of the room and states they will return soon. Recording messages on a cassette recorder can have the same reassuring effect and give you some space to yourself.

MARCH 3

Everyone has unique talents, strengths and weaknesses. Making comparisons is not a wise thing to do. Comparing human qualities is impossible. No two individuals are alike enough to compare. No two people have ever experienced the exact same things in life. We are each one unparalleled, rare and unusual. I try not to compare myself to anyone else.

Today's Tip: Allow your loved one time to process what you say to her. Don't be anxious for a quick response. Avoid pronouns. Use names. It's less confusing. Your patience and consideration will make communication easier for both of you.

MARCH 4

I don't have to do the things I am doing. I want to do them! I don't give out of obligation. I want to give. It's my turn to give. It is what I choose to do and it feels good. I am motivated by love.

Today's Tip: Having order and a schedule in your life can help with daily activities. Routines might help your loved one function in a more normal and familiar manner, but try not to be so rigid that there is no allowance for spontaneity or creativity. Adjustments in schedules are often appropriate to avoid agitation or boredom.

MARCH 5

Laughter is good for me. Sometimes tears are, too. There are times when nothing else helps like a good cry. I might need to do this all by myself or in the confidence and presence of a trusted friend. When pressure builds, tears are often the release and relief I need. Afterward I blow my nose, dry my eyes, and face the world anew — refreshed by the experience.

Today's Tip: Consistency in your life can help your loved one feel secure and confident. It may help him retain certain memory skills longer. Use the same door when going outside, sit at the same places at mealtime, and do some of the same activities every day.

MARCH 6

Trust is having a firm belief in something or someone. I trust in God. I trust others and others place their trust in me. People need people. I am proud to be trustworthy and I'm fortunate to have reliable family and friends in whom I can trust. We can depend upon one another.

Today's Tip: Some AD patients form close bonds with other AD patients they meet at day care or through other activities. They may even hold hands, walk hand-in-hand, or kiss each other. If you observe this behavior in your loved one, try not to take it personally. Your loved one is not aware it could upset you.

MARCH 7

Having beauty around me gives me joy. I don't have to spend money to create a pleasing atmosphere for me and the people I love. There is beauty in a clean room, garden flowers on the table, and soothing music emanating from the radio.

Today's Tip: It is normal for your loved one to ask you the same questions over and over again. She is having trouble with her memory and may be feeling insecure. Be considerate and reassuring when you answer her. Giving the same answer to a commonly repeated question may help her remember the answer herself.

MARCH 8

I'm a good listener. I listen to my loved ones and my friends. They deserve my time and my undivided attention. It is one of the highest forms of love. Listening is a way to show I care. I also care about myself. I listen to the little voice inside me telling me I am lovable and I love myself.

Today's Tip: If your loved one sometimes uses words that are inappropriate or don't seem to fit, take time to figure out what he really means. He may form the wrong sound and the word he uses rhymes with the word he really wants to say. You may try pointing to an object and asking, "Is this what you're talking about?" Or, if he can, ask him to point to what he's talking about.

MARCH 9

Whenever possible I stay away from people who constantly exhibit a negative outlook on life. I have concern for them but overexposure to them can be harmful to my emotional well-being. I prefer the company of spiritually healthy individuals who see the positives in any given situation. I try to be one of those individuals myself!

Today's Tip: Watching children at play and hearing them laugh can be a wonderful activity for your loved one. She may remember her childhood more easily than she remembers recent times. Encourage conversation about her childhood.

MARCH 10

Life is not without pain. Pain cannot be avoided. It is the manner in which I face pain that matters. Do I let it have power over me? Or do I gain strength in the way I handle pain?

Today's Tip: Financial matters can be very disturbing to your loved one. You need to reassure him that everything is fine. If he wants to have control over money, try to change the subject. If he wants to see his money, you might say, "Your money is safe in the bank." Get good legal advice and make any changes that might be necessary in your bank accounts and financial affairs. An attorney well versed in elder law and your current situation should advise you regarding important legal documents you may need such as a Durable Power of Attorney.

MARCH 11

I am giving my best effort. I will continue to give my best effort until it is not enough. I realize there may come a time when circumstances beyond my control call for considering other choices. When that time comes I will be able to give my best effort in new ways knowing I have always done what is best for my loved one and myself.

Today's Tip: Dementia patients who enjoyed reading but can no longer read words successfully seem to get pleasure looking at large picture books which contain few written words. There are many readily available picture books of places, things, and famous people. They can provide peaceful enjoyment. They may also inspire conversation and memories.

MARCH 12

Criticism is crippling. Praise is uplifting. When I commend someone I show approval. Kind words of appreciation are encouraging. They go a long way in helping to make someone's day a little easier.

Today's Tip: If your loved one is disoriented upon waking in the mornings, don't rush her. Take time for a good conversation before breakfast. Keep things quiet and low-key while she adjusts to being awake.

MARCH 13

I am learning things about myself I never knew before. I am more resilient than I thought. I have become creative and imaginative. I am able to do things I didn't know I could do. I'm more self-reliant and self-confident. I'm okay!

Today's Tip: If your loved one is adamant about not wanting to take a shower or bath, don't force something that could be dangerous for both of you. Thorough sponge baths may be the solution for a while. Continue to offer showers in a friendly non-controlling and non-judgmental manner. The resistance may just suddenly disappear.

MARCH 14

Being brave means to be courageous. I know my loved one is brave. Every day he faces his losses. He has feelings and exasperations. It must be painful for him when he is unable to communicate his feelings to me in the ways he used to. He makes valiant efforts. I am proud of him and I tell him so.

Today's Tip: You most likely know your loved one better than anyone else does. His body language probably speaks to you as well as his verbal communication once did. Your close attention to his body language can help you determine his feelings, emotions, and reactions to things.

MARCH 15

When things get tense, I need to slow down. Sometimes deep breathing exercises help. Sometimes a shoulder or neck exercise loosens me up. Sitting down and enjoying a big glass of water can be refreshing. Taking a break and then beginning again at a slower pace eases the tension for me.

Today's Tip: Some caregivers find they prepare answers in advance to anticipated questions. They plan the right words to achieve the desired results. Resistance to day care can be met with, "Today is a special day at day care." It may sound a little devious or a distortion of reality, but after all, isn't every day a special day?

MARCH 16

Keeping a daily journal is fulfilling and therapeutic for me. Some days I have more time to write and more to say than other days, but I try to write often. I am honest and sincere in expressing my feelings and observations. Today it helps me. Someday it may help someone else!

Today's Tip: If you and your loved one enjoyed playing cards together in the past, continue playing cards with her. Cheerfully offer help if she needs it. You can count her hand and yours. Large playing cards might help too. Card playing could still be a pleasant pastime.

MARCH 17

Every person has his own dignity. My loved one's dignity can be preserved and treated with respect at all times. I am sensitive to his right to maintain his pride and dignity. I am careful of him.

Today's Tip: Cutting your loved one's food into bite size pieces may make mealtime easier for him. Don't cut it at the table. This is embarrassing and demeaning. When you eat out, quietly explain to the waiter you would like both of your meals pre-cut in the kitchen before he brings the food to the table.

MARCH 18

Humility is the realization God loves each and every one of us equally. No one person is any more special to God than their earthly brother. When I remember this I get things into perspective quickly! I understand the person at the other end of the phone may just be having a bad day. I have bad days, too. I exercise compassion with a word of encouragement and kindness.

Today's Tip: Be sure to use lots of moisturizing lotion on your loved one's skin after bathing. She might like it applied again at bedtime with a soothing massage. Don't forget to be good to your skin too!

MARCH 19

Life always looks better with the dawn of a fresh new day. I will enjoy the newness of this day from beginning to end. Spring is fast approaching. I look for signs of new life in nature. Hints of green and birds returning are a beautiful sight.

Today's Tip: If your loved one doesn't recognize some family members and friends, houseguests could present a problem. He might be threatened by them and feel they are intruders. Awareness of this possibility and some advance preparation or alternate plans on your part could help avoid a difficult situation.

MARCH 20

I don't try to be right all the time. I lose some battles. Sometimes it's easier that way. When I admit I can be wrong I respect the fact someone else can be right. Often there is humor in a situation when I admit I goofed! I am the only person I permit myself to laugh at.

Today's Tip: Try to incorporate your loved one in your day without controlling or forcing her. Encourage her help in the things you need to do. She might get satisfaction dusting the furniture while you vacuum. Make tasks like shopping a fun excursion.

MARCH 21

Old unresolved hurts can come out in times of stress and tension. It is always best to deal with a problem when it occurs. It is no longer appropriate to discuss old hurts with my loved one and I don't want to blurt out something under stress I might regret. If I am harboring an old hurt or resentment, I need to discuss it with someone I trust. Getting an old problem out in the open usually takes away its importance.

Today's Tip: A baby doll can be a great source of enjoyment and comfort for some AD patients. They lovingly carry, care for, and talk to their baby.

MARCH 22

Every family has a delicate balance. I am careful not to upset this balance even though some circumstances have changed. Out of necessity new roles have been created. I am trying not to change anyone's place in the family structure. I respect the family order and constantly find creative and loving ways to maintain it.

Today's Tip: Try to preserve your loved one's comfort level. Respect his privacy and modesty as much as safety and cleanliness will allow. If he requires help, talk to him in comforting words. Explain your understanding of his discomfort in the situation. Consider a visiting nurse a few times a week for bathing. If he is modest about undressing in front of you, try undressing him from the back. Avoid mirrors when undressing him.

MARCH 23

Fear can cause people to be suspicious, anxious, or timid. Some people react to fear with panic. Some strike out at what they think is causing their fear. Others may try to run away from whatever frightens them. We all react in different ways depending on our personalities and experiences. By understanding her reactions to fear, I am more aware of what frightens my loved one. This knowledge helps avoid many disturbing situations.

Today's Tip: You may not be able to figure out what causes some of your loved one's fears. Try to keep her environment as simple, peaceful, and familiar as possible. Changing furniture can be frightening. New locations for familiar things might cause panic if she can't find them.

MARCH 24

I have decided to be loving. Love is a conscious decision. It is something I am committed to. Sometimes I may not feel loving, but my loving actions take over and before I know it I also feel loving. Others benefit from my decision and so do I.

Today's Tip: Just as your loved one's body language reveals his feelings to you, he is aware of your body language as well. We all give non-verbal messages to each other by the way we look and by the things we do. The look of love is calm and supportive. We can do things like hugging, kissing, and smiling to communicate love.

MARCH 25

My attitude is contagious. Almost everyone I come in contact with today can catch it. Would I rather be surrounded by cheerful attitudes or dreadful attitudes? It could all start with whatever attitude I have. I'll most definitely choose to have a cheerful attitude!

Today's Tip: If your loved one is having difficulty locating some things, try putting labels or signs on drawers, cupboards, and doors. They can be big printed words or pictures of objects if the printed word no longer has meaning for her. Photographs of familiar objects pasted to where they belong often helps. If she is able to cook or help in the kitchen, consider putting items into clear plastic containers.

MARCH 26

I no longer strive for perfection. Peace and serenity are my new objectives. They make a great deal more sense to me than perfection. What is perfect, anyway? Somehow perfection is never attainable. I have found inner peace and serenity are attainable when I take one day at a time. I am discovering what really matters.

Today's Tip: If your loved one insists on doing something that is not harmful, let him do it. He may get satisfaction and a feeling of independence from doing it. You'll help maintain inner peace for both of you by not opposing him.

MARCH 27

Compliments are important. We all need them. They lift us up. Today I will remember to compliment someone. I will start with my loved one. I will compliment her on something of importance to her. I remember the compliments she used to give me and know she would express them if she could.

Today's Tip: Shoes with laces may be difficult for your loved one. They can be dangerous if they become untied. Slip-on shoes and shoes with Velcro fasteners are easier and safer.

MARCH 28

Other people are important and necessary in my life. My loved one, family, and friends should all know they are special to me. Sometimes I appear to have everything in control when I am actually struggling inside like everyone else. It is not a sign of weakness to admit I need their support.

Today's Tip: When you need a hug, tell your loved one. He may yearn to know you want his affection as much as he does yours.

MARCH 29

My relationship with someone is my connection to them. How good the connection is has a great deal to do with my relationship with God, followed by my relationship with myself. The quality of every other relationship is in direct proportion to the first two. If I find I am having difficulty in my relationships with others I'd be wise to try to improve my connection to God and to myself. My other relationships might just miraculously improve!

Today's Tip: Some quiet time for yourself every day is a must. Thirty minutes a day is great, but whatever time you can manage in a daily meditative retreat can work wonders.

MARCH 30

I am not afraid of life. Exposure to life involves taking risks. Every day I take risks of one sort or another. I refuse to sit in frozen anxiety when life hands me a new problem. I will risk trying a new solution. If it doesn't work, I'll try another!

Today's Tip: Chairs with armrests and high firm seats may be easier for your loved one to get in and out of. When he goes to sit down, make sure he is close enough to the chair. The back of his knees should touch the chair before he sits.

MARCH 31

I accept other people the way they are. I don't expect them to be like me. I respect individualities. Our differences fascinate me. I learn from others. Others learn from me. How dull life would be if we were all alike!

Today's Tip: Your loved one may be unsure and shuffle when she walks. Provide handrails where possible and remove dangerous throw rugs. Sturdy shoes with rubber soles will help her feel more steady. When helping her walk, have her take your arm and hold your arm close to your body. Walk at her pace — not yours.

APRIL

APRIL 1

I am joyful when I give love. I am not so narrow-minded to expect I will get back in the exact same ways I give. I receive in many unexpected ways. The joy I get from giving love is one of the beautiful ways love is returned to me. We are all beloved children of God.

Today's Tip: When your loved one is searching for a word while talking, he might appreciate your help in supplying it. Be cheerful, not impatient. In the same manner try offering the correct word if he uses an incorrect word. Don't persist in providing the correct word if he objects.

APRIL 2

I am not nearly as concerned about how others treat me as I am about how I treat others. My responsibility lies in my actions alone, not in the actions of others. I cannot tell other people how to conduct themselves. Perhaps my acts of courtesy and kindness will serve as a model they might choose to copy.

Today's Tip: Try using a sturdy plastic chair in the shower stall as your relative may feel more secure when sitting. Some caregivers place the back of the chair facing the shower nozzle. Water on the back can be more comfortable and less frightening than on the front of the body. When helping, be sure to tell her what you are doing, step by step.

APRIL 3

I ask for God's help every day. He sends it in many ways throughout the day. His help comes in the inner peace he gives me, in the supportive friends he sends me, in the resources he supplies, and in countless unexpected ways each day. My strength comes from God.

Today's Tip: You may find your loved one starting projects and never finishing them. He might stop in the middle because he can't remember how to finish properly or because something else entered his mind. His attention span could be getting shorter. Don't encourage a project or activity he cannot complete.

APRIL 4

It is important to have a doctor who converses with me in language and terms I understand. It is essential he has the time to talk with me and listen to my concerns. He must be current on AD and AD research. I expect him to keep up on the latest medications available, their advantages and their side effects. He must be considerate of the effects the disease has on my loved one and on me as the primary caregiver.

Today's Tip: There may be several explanations for why some AD patients wander. If your loved one wanders aimlessly she may need more vigorous exercise or more stimulating activities. If she seems in search of a place or home, give her frequent reassurance of her whereabouts. Safety is of prime importance. An identification bracelet is a must.

APRIL 5

Although some forms of change can frighten my loved one, we both need a little change in routine once in a while. I have become a pretty good judge of what forms of change disturb him. My presence, constant reassurance, and approval help make small breaks from the norm enjoyable. A picnic in the park or a quiet lunch at our favorite restaurant today could be fun!

Today's Tip: Suggesting a selection from the menu or telling your loved one what you are considering having can help him feel more comfortable in a restaurant. He shouldn't be faced with a lot of choices and he may be unable to understand the menu himself. Put him at ease and you'll both enjoy yourselves.

APRIL 6

Seeing other people is good for all of us. Family and friends can boost my loved one's spirits and mine too. Today I'll reach out and make social plans we are all comfortable with. If I attend a social function, I'll make sure that my relative spends time with someone whose company he enjoys.

Today's Tip: The friends you make at your support group meetings may be the caregivers of friends your loved one makes at day care. You might want to get your families together socially. If some social skills have been forgotten, everyone understands.

APRIL 7

Sometimes I have to remind myself it is normal to get tired. Taking care of myself and another person can be exhausting -- physically and emotionally. It's all right to admit I'm tired. It is also all right to do something about it. In fact, it is imperative I do something about it. Thinking of myself is not selfish. It is normal and necessary.

Today's Tip: Don't try to overcompensate to make everything okay. Everything is not okay and whatever you do won't make it okay. Know you are doing your best. Don't let yourself get sick by overcompensating.

APRIL 8

Feelings are feelings. They are not right or wrong. They just are. If I face my feelings and accept them, I am healthier. I go on and I accept myself. It's okay to realize I might have some feelings of loss, guilt, or sadness. I don't let them take over — I just acknowledge them.

Today's Tip: The activities of daily living — bathing, dressing, toileting — are the causes of most caregiver stress. Know what kind of help is available and take advantage of it. Home care may be obtainable through community services, governmental programs, volunteers, churches or private agencies.

APRIL 9

When I don't understand someone's actions, I try to put myself in their place and imagine what they must be feeling or going through. I try to see things from their perspective. It generally helps both of us when I stop and do this.

Today's Tip: Everyone feels better when they look good. Making sure your loved one's hair and nails are well groomed can do a lot for her spirits. If you don't feel adept in this area, seek the assistance of a close relative, friend, or professional.

APRIL 10

I must admit some of my loved one's actions embarrass me. I know he doesn't do inappropriate things intentionally. He is most likely embarrassed also. The best thing I can do is reassure him of my love and understanding. I am learning to anticipate some of the things that cause embarrassing actions or outbursts. At times I can successfully stop them from occurring.

Today's Tip: Some caregivers carry calling cards explaining their companion is memory impaired and to please excuse any unusual behavior. They discreetly hand them to store sales people or anyone they come in contact with who does not know their loved one. Some AD support centers have the cards printed and available to caregivers at no cost.

APRIL 11

Every day I am called upon to be creative. Opportunities present themselves in the form of minor problems. I manage to keep the problems minor by facing them head on. I try to remain calm, practical, and realistic when challenges arise. I expect them. I accept them as invitations to grow. I work my way through to creative solutions!

Today's Tip: Reduce clutter. Make sure carpet is firmly secured. Safe walking paths can be identified by signs or arrows. Reflective tape along baseboards and handrails can identify the route to the bathroom.

APRIL 12

There is a delicate balance to the caregiving of another adult. I encourage my loved one to be independent. At the same time I have concern for her safety and well-being. It is important to urge her participation in tasks and activities within her capabilities. She needs assurance of her value as an adult member of society.

Today's Tip: You can use short simple sentences without talking down to your loved one. Avoid judgmental words and criticism. Respecting her as an adult will encourage self-confidence.

APRIL 13

I don't worry about the future. Nothing is certain. I prefer to live in today, but I do need to be prepared for future possibilities. I have made provisions based on professional legal and financial guidance. Well thought out preparation today could help tomorrow.

Today's Tip: Living wills and surrogate health care forms can differ from state to state. Homestead property laws and laws pertaining to the sale of jointly held property may not be the same in each state. The ability to sell joint holdings and stocks should be covered in a Durable Power of Attorney, but your state may require a specific Power of Attorney for the sale of real estate. Make sure you have a competent lawyer practicing in the state in which your loved one is a legal resident.

APRIL 14

Every day contains a mixture of good and bad experiences. Life has two opposing forces -- positive and negative. I have a choice of which one has the controlling effect over me. They are both powerful and compelling. I am much better off when I concentrate on the positives and allow them to have the more profound influence on my life.

Today's Tip: Sit directly across from your loved one at mealtime so he can copy you. Use deep plates or plates with lips. Offer lots of finger foods if utensils are a problem. Turn his plate when one side is empty. Avoid distractions during mealtime. If he stops eating, he may not start again.

APRIL 15

When someone is having a difficult time, their behavior is apt to be difficult. Other people need our love most when they are the most unlovable. This is the real test of love. It is easy to love someone under the best of circumstances, but when the chips are down only unconditional love shows up and stays!

Today's Tip: Avoiding caffeine and cutting down on excessive sugar intake may help reduce restlessness, pacing, and sleepless nights. You might want to try serving your loved one decaffeinated teas and coffees.

APRIL 16

I don't concentrate on what I've lost, I focus on what I have left. It's the age-old question of seeing a glass as being half-full or half-empty. I prefer to see it as half-full. I'm free to enjoy what I have and I'm much richer in spirit!

Today's Tip: Make sure your loved one gets three healthy meals a day and three good snacks. Offer liquids frequently to avoid dehydration. Don't forget you need the same balanced diet as your loved one!

APRIL 17

To respond to someone else's needs effectively, I am not necessarily losing part of myself. I am finding a part of myself I would not find in any other way. I reach down into some unselfish part of me that has been unknown until now. I've found a buried treasure we can both partake of.

Today's Tip: The use of commercial child-proof doorknob covers might discourage wandering. Be aware some AD loved ones can open anything if they want to!

APRIL 18

I cannot be all things to all people. If I am feeling pulled and worn thin, I need to be honest with myself and with others. I must do some re-evaluating of my priorities, my time, and my abilities. Everyone has their limitations and I cannot be pushed beyond mine.

Today's Tip: Purchasing spare sets of frequently lost items could buy a lot of peace!

APRIL 19

I consoled my children when they were frightened. I took time to discover a new awareness with them. I shared the awe they felt when studying a wild flower. I walked hand in hand with them. I laughed freely with them. In many ways I have similar opportunities today. My loved one trusts me and shares his new childlike world with me.

Today's Tip: Short visits with grandchildren or neighborhood youngsters might delight your loved one. Playing childhood games or sharing ice cream can be a pleasant experience.

APRIL 20

My support group is a lifeline I reach out for and grab hold of. Some days it is the foghorn I strain to hear as I make my way through this fog. The people there are like beacons of light in a lighthouse. They give me hope when I need it. My cares and fears are safe with them. They understand because they travel through these same uncharted waters.

Today's Tip: Bright colors and busy prints can distract and over stimulate some patients. Placemats, tablecloths, and dishes in colorful patterns may distract your loved one from eating.

APRIL 21

Sometimes I find myself missing my loved one even though he is right here with me. Or, is he? There are days when I'm sure some alien person has taken up residence inside him. Then, at other times I see him clearly. He is still in there. The reality is that he will never be a stranger. A new bond is forming, in some ways a stronger one.

Today's Tip: Your family may not live near you. Distance can keep them from realizing what you experience on a daily basis. Suggest that they attend a support group in their area. They will better understand your situation and feelings. Also it will help them deal with their feelings and provide answers to questions they may have.

APRIL 22

Why do I feel guilty? I'm doing my best and deep down, I know I'm also doing enough. I sometimes feel badly knowing I may not be able to care for my loved one at home forever. I need to remind myself that I am not responsible for the changes brought about by the progression of this disease.

Today's Tip: Unfortunately, guilt is a commonly held emotion among caregivers. The dictionary defines guilt as the fact of having committed some offense, or the feeling that you are to blame for something. Neither definition applies to you. You aren't doing anything wrong. You are helping someone. You are not to blame for the disease. You are doing everything within your power.

APRIL 23

My loved one teaches me many things. He lives in the moment. The passage of time has lost its meaning for him. He enjoys things as they happen. It's a fresh quality I seem to have forgotten until now.

Today's Tip: Some caregivers find shopping with their loved one presents problems. Wandering away and shop-lifting are not uncommon actions for dementia patients. Both behaviors are hard to control. Day care, home health care, or an understanding friend may provide time for you to shop alone. Remember, some stores and pharmacies still deliver.

APRIL 24

I just need someone to listen. I don't need advice. I need a heart that listens. I just want a friend to stand by me — someone to hold my hand and understand. I will seek out that friend today.

Today's Tip: Many caregivers find they lose some old friends. Friends don't know what to do. They think they need to have answers for you. They can't relate to your new circumstances. Some old friends do stay close. New friends at AD support groups will stand by you. And don't forget, God always listens.

APRIL 25

Rage is not a behavior I am accustomed to. Recently my loved one has exhibited a wrath I've never seen in her before. She must be as uncomfortable with it as I am. I struggle to find the cause of it. I search for ways to curb her stress and discourage violence of any kind.

Today's Tip: When dealing with a memory impaired person, logic doesn't necessarily work. Sometimes it even helps to bend the truth a little if you know it will achieve the desired results. As the primary caregiver, you will learn what works for you and your loved one.

APRIL 26

There are days I long for some time to myself. When I get it, I don't know what to do with it! I can't remember all the things I wanted to do. Or there are so many projects and activities to choose from that I can't make a choice. It even feels strange to be by myself. This probably means it's been too long since I've had any time to myself. I need to schedule it on a more regular basis.

Today's Tip: If your loved one develops an obsession with gadgets, locks, or taking things apart, you'll probably end up with broken items and repair bills. Realistic toys and old items purchased at garage sales can be substituted for things you don't want to replace, repair, or reassemble.

APRIL 27

It saddens me that I can no longer share favorite memories with my loved one. But I treasure them and they still bring me pleasure. I will pass them on to my family through dialog, picture albums, and perhaps my journal. It is something I can do for my loved one and those dear to us.

Today's Tip: The words to old favorite songs linger long after other memories have faded. Sing-a-longs can be fun and meaningful. Your loved one may surprise you as he joins in with all the words!

APRIL 28

I've become a peacemaker. I have learned many ways of keeping the peace. Sometimes I am troubled over the responsibility for harmony between my loved one and other family members. I must remember that family members need to take responsibility for their own relationships. Maintaining peace sometimes makes me crazy. Other times it keeps me sane. At any rate, I've developed a peaceful attitude!

Today's Tip: In the early stages of AD, your loved one could have trouble taking telephone messages accurately. She may even have difficulty dialing the phone or she might call her own number repeatedly. If she dials numbers randomly, discourage her from using the phone as people sometimes run up large telephone bills this way. One gentleman dialed his Social Security Number and someone answered!

APRIL 29

I can be my loved one's memory. He seems to trust me with it. I keep it safe in my heart. My loving actions toward him reflect the beautiful times we shared together. I can make sure my memory of this time is beautiful too, in its own tender way.

Today's Tip: A family pet often senses feelings, fears, and changes. Changes in the behavior of a family member can alter the behavior of a pet. Just having this awareness can help you understand if your family pet seems uneasy around your AD loved one. The pet may also sense something is wrong and be very protective and stay close to the loved one.

APRIL 30

Emotional pain is not so different from physical pain. Pain is pain. When sensing pain in others some people run away. Do they think it is contagious? Do they run because they can't do anything about it? When the pain is personal, running is not an option. I choose to stand when I'm in pain and when those I love are in pain. I won't run and I won't lay down. I will work through it.

Today's Tip: You may have to keep colognes and aftershaves out of reach if your loved one cannot distinguish between what is a beverage and what is not.

MAY

MAY 1

Some days are better than others! My loved one has some good days and some difficult days. His world is changing. He travels through stages of unrest and stages of tranquility. Many days are filled with both.

Today's Tip: Sometimes the best gift we can give someone is our presence. Spending time shows we care. Just sitting beside your loved one is reassuring. Closeness can speak volumes of love to someone who is hurting.

MAY 2

Letting God be in charge helps me each day. By turning my fears over to him I more easily determine what I can do and what I cannot do. I'm not successful when I repeatedly take back what I give him. If I let go and let God do his part, I am free to do my part successfully. It's a great partnership!

Today's Tip: The first sign of incontinence is usually urinary. If your loved one exhibits any urinary problems have his physician check to make sure it's not an infection before you assume incontinence. The onset of incontinence can be postponed by following a routine bathroom schedule. Proper observation will help you determine the appropriate time intervals.

MAY 3

I'll never forget my first AD support group meeting. I looked around at each face and wondered where they got their strength. I've come to realize it comes from sharing with each other. I'm grateful to those who led the way. They encouraged me to share my fears. They shared their experiences with me. They made a difference in my life. Now, when newcomers join us, I take their hand and tell them they've come to the right place.

Today's Tip: Joining a support group may be difficult at first. Many members suggest attending at least six meetings before making any judgments about their value.

MAY 4

The times when I have been absolutely certain about something are the times I have usually been proven wrong. When I chose to go it alone, I got nowhere. I can't expect to successfully deal with this disease alone. I need the help of caring family and friends, current information, and all the resources I can get my hands on.

Today's Tip: Sundowning is a term which refers to the perplexing behavior changes that occur in some Alzheimer's patients after the sun goes down. Perhaps less light makes them feel insecure. Weariness may bring on the changes, or they may be caused by a change in household activities late in the day. If you experience restlessness and anxiety in your loved one as the day wears on, be sensitive to the possible causes and ways you can help him feel secure.

MAY 5

I can see a problem better when I let go of it. If I hold it tightly in my fist I can't see it. I must open my hand. In doing so I get it out in the light. I can release it by sharing with others and by giving it to God. I don't have to try to solve all my problems by myself.

Today's Tip: Consider sitting or kneeling when talking to your loved one who is seated in a chair or wheelchair. You will be at eye level and can be better understood. The gesture is loving and considerate. It also makes you seem less powerful.

MAY 6

No one has all the answers. My caregiver friends don't. My doctor doesn't and I certainly don't. But we all work together and we don't stop trying. We share new information. We share our frustrations, trials, errors and successes. It's team work!

Today's Tip: When they are unable to locate the toilet in time, dementia patients will sometimes use an inappropriate object as a substitute. If your loved one gets up during the night and has difficulty finding the bathroom, consider placing a portable toilet next to her bed. Keep a light on in the bedroom.

I believe in myself. I am meeting constantly changing needs. I meet them in different ways. Some things I handle myself. Some I handle by asking for the assistance of other capable people. I have learned to use all the resources at hand. I am a more effective caregiver when I can see the whole picture. I am realistic in the ways I manage the ever-changing demands of caregiving.

Today's Tip: Don't wear yourself out trying to do everything. If you need help in house maintenance, yard work, driving, caregiving — whatever — make sure you get the help you need. A primary caregiver must learn to delegate. Don't be a martyr!

MAY 8

Some of my greatest support comes from people I hardly knew. I am secretly embarrassed because in the past I overlooked their loyalty. I expected support from some friends who have become scarce. We find out who our true friends are when we most need them. I have learned a good lesson in becoming a better friend.

Today's Tip: Some communities have support groups for patients in the early stages of AD. If this applies and your loved one is interested, check to see if one is offered locally. Don't push if he isn't interested.

MAY 9

I need to recharge often. Caregiving drains me. Life is a system of deposits and withdrawals. I must refill on a regular basis. I do this by maintaining interests and activities that nourish me. It is unrealistic to think I can totally put my life and my individuality on hold. I will have nothing to give if I become an empty shell. I owe it to my loved one to replenish my inner self by participating in activities that fulfill me.

Today's Tip: A little time away from your loved one will make you appreciate her more when you're together. Time away from you on a regular basis can help prevent over-dependence on her part. Trust other capable and dependable people to care for her while you recharge!

MAY 10

Forgiveness is so cleansing! I forgive my loved one for his unpredictable behavior. I know he can't help it. Starting today I'll give myself the same courtesy. The mistakes I make are not intentional. I need to forget them and forgive myself. I know my God and my loved one forgive and forget my mistakes.

Today's Tip: Many household items can be used to create stimulating games or activities. Buttons can be sorted. Playing cards can be matched. Tennis balls can be rolled or tossed into a waste basket.

MAY 11

Life doesn't always go the way I would like. It helps when I don't take it personally. If I see myself as a victim, I will be a victim. Instead I choose to make the best of whatever situation I am in. I recognize what I cannot control and what I can control. I see myself as a viable participant in a real world.

Today's Tip: Pacing can be the result of restlessness or a need to be active. If your loved one paces without showing signs of frustration or anxiety, provide him with a safe secure pacing route in your home or enclosed yard. The routine, the exercise, and the feeling of independence should be good for him.

MAY 12

In the midst of turmoil and unrest I am experiencing an inner tranquility. My own feelings run deep. I look beyond actions and behaviors. I feel. I let my loved one know I understand her feelings.

Today's Tip: It is not unusual for an AD loved one to accuse their spouse of infidelity. This is generally not based on any facts. It might come from fear of being left. They may feel insecure about not being the person they used to be. They might fear losing their spouse's love. Some cannot distinguish between reality and television programs. They may put themselves into the plot of a story involving infidelity.

MAY 13

My loved one and I always brought out the best in each other. We continue to do that. Life's changes have not robbed us of this special quality. We still share it. His caregiving needs bring out the best in me. My love and support encourage him to be the best he can be.

Today's Tip: Involve your loved one in situations and activities that are the most failure-free for him. Maintaining his adult dignity is of utmost importance. If he functions well socially, encourage general conversations with casual acquaintances. Brief pleasant encounters can go a long way in promoting his self-esteem.

MAY 14

Experience is often the best teacher. Everyday I have more to build from. I learn from my own experiences. I also learn when others share with me. I benefit from their experiences as well as my own. Help from others can come in the form of books, newsletters, or the personal sharing of other caregivers.

Today's Tip: Your attic or storage space is probably filled with old belongings and mementos which could be meaningful to your loved one. Bring some out now. They may bring back pleasant memories. Having them to hold and look at might provide joy and comfort. Keep favorite objects out where she can enjoy them.

MAY 15

I cannot dwell on my strengths alone. I will not grow if I continue to overlook my weak spots. Ignoring them will not make them disappear. I need to work on them. Changing weaknesses into strengths promotes my growth. I am made up of strengths and weaknesses. Hard work and discipline are required of me if I am to grow.

Today's Tip: If your loved one wanders, make sure your local law agency is aware of his dementia. His confused behavior or lack of cooperation could present a problem if stopped by authorities. Make sure you have a recent picture and an accurate written description of him on hand. Know what he is wearing at all times.

MAY 16

When I get my secrets out in the open they lose their power. The longer I keep a troubling thought inside me the larger it becomes. It can shrink to normal size if I share it with someone I trust. In fact, normal is the optimum word here — I find out I am normal. Others have struggled with a similar secret. I am no different!

Today's Tip: If you and your loved one enjoy the outdoors, try planting a garden together. Working with the soil, getting fresh air and communing with nature is refreshing and uplifting.

MAY 17

I have hope. It is not hope that everything will suddenly be perfect. It is hope that I will come through this not-so-perfect time a better person. I hope my presence will make a difference for my loved one and for others.

Today's Tip: Many caregivers attend church or synagogue with their family member. If your loved one fidgets or talks to others when silence is appropriate, have him sit in the aisle seat where you will be the only one next to him. Alternatively, try sitting in the back row in case you choose to leave early. Bring a small soft object to keep his hands busy, something that will not roll or make noise if dropped.

MAY 18

My loved one sends me messages I need to hear. They are not always verbal or audible. I must be attentive to the messages she works so hard to send me. If I am thinking ahead to tomorrow or trying to tell her what I think, I may miss what she so desperately wants to communicate. I will work on listening with more than my ears.

Today's Tip: Display favorite sayings, quotes, slogans, or prayers on the refrigerator, on mirrors, or wherever you will see them throughout the day. You'll be surprised how comforting and inspiring they can be.

MAY 19

Reality for my loved one often differs from the reality I know. His world is changing. What is real to him is not always real to me. I respect his view of reality. Trying to talk him out of it doesn't work. I comfort him when he is frightened. I tell him I understand. I am pleased when something in his reality brings him pleasure.

Today's Tip: Your loved one may see and hear people and things you can't see or hear. He might carry on conversations with people who are not actually in the room. Sometimes he may misinterpret real things due to poor eyesight or hearing. You will probably be able to determine whether he is experiencing hallucinations or not. Like any other changes in behavior, consult with his doctor to help determine the possible causes and ways of handling them.

MAY 20

Let go. Let God. Let live. These three slogans have become quite meaningful to me. I let go of my hold on the things I cannot control. I let God have control over them. I let my loved one be herself within the margin of safety.

Today's Tip: If your loved one insists upon holding onto an idea that is not based on reality, telling her she is mistaken probably won't change her mind. She may actually believe something to be true that is not. Occasionally these delusions may make her sad, depressed, or suspicious. When this is the case, comfort her and try to introduce a more pleasant thought or distraction.

MAY 21

I have discovered a beautiful form of meditation in times of distress. I ask God to calm my heart and replace any troubling thought with a pleasant picture. Concentrating on a pleasing thought or object removes the distressing thought. The short intervention calms me and I return to reality refreshed.

Today's Tip: Ask family children and teens not to leave shoes, books, sports equipment or toys laying around where they could cause an accident.

MAY 22

I try not to overdo my role as a caregiver. I remind myself I operate in other areas, too. Balance is still called for in my life. I have family, community, and social circles in which I am required to function as well. I try not to overdo any obligation. I strive for a workable balance in my life.

Today's Tip: Don't break contact with others. You are not being disloyal to your loved one by maintaining relationships that have always been important to you. You need the balance to preserve a good outlook and keep a proper perspective.

MAY 23

I'm working on removing the word *should* from my vocabulary. I try to refrain from telling my loved one what he *should* be doing or how he *should* be doing it. I've also come to realize I'm more content when I don't tell myself I *should* be doing something. The word implies an obligation. It lays unreal expectations and unnecessary burdens on both of us, which could cause feelings of guilt.

Today's Tip: Don't pull or tug at someone with dementia to get him to move or go somewhere with you. His reaction could be catastrophic. Also it's not a good idea to move someone in a wheelchair without first explaining where and why you are moving him.

MAY 24

Sometimes things don't get better, they just get different. AD has stages and they aren't all predictable or the same for everyone. There is no reliable time factor for estimating the length of any phase. The only thing that is certain is change. I keep a good sense of humor and I see the value in the saying, "This too will pass."

Today's Tip: When her loved one insisted he wanted to go home despite the fact he was home, one caregiver had success in offering to drive him there. He was content to look out the car window searching for his house as she drove him around. When they'd arrive back at their home he often told her to turn into the driveway. Sometimes he did not recognize the house. She would suggest it looked like a nice house and why not stop there. This routine worked for a long time. She was helping him and he appreciated it.

MAY 25

I am often overwhelmed. Some tasks seem too big. I have learned to step back. I survey the situation. I assess whether I can realistically handle it. I decide if I want to handle it or not. If my decision is to go ahead, I proceed one step at a time. If I decide not to do it and it is something that needs to be done, I find help.

Today's Tip: Your loved one might repeat an activity many times during the day. She probably forgets she has already done it. If it is something that can be repeated without doing any harm, let her do it. It is most likely an activity she still performs successfully and she gets satisfaction from doing it.

MAY 26

One of the things I am learning about change is that it's okay for me to change my mind. Nothing is written in stone. Sometimes I have to make changes in midstream. Things change from day to day. What worked yesterday may no longer apply. I am not embarrassed to change my mind if yesterday's decision doesn't fit today's situation.

Today's Tip: If your loved one asks the same question over and over again, you are probably tired of answering it. Sometimes it helps to write a large note with the answer on it. Kindly hand him the note every time he asks the question. You may wish to give him the note to keep on his lap or make a sign out of it and post it where he can see it. Refer to it whenever he asks. Posting it may also keep him from asking since he can see the answer. It could be reassuring for him.

I just accept there is no rhyme or reason for some of my loved one's behavior. No matter how hard I try to figure some things out, I can't find a reasonable explanation. My logic does not always apply to her logic. I have learned to roll with the punches. I help her have a good day and I no longer measure her behavior with my old yardstick.

Today's Tip: Often AD patients in moderately severe stages of the disease display moments of lucidity with no apparent explanation. Enjoy such moments with them.

MAY 28

I know my own limitations. I recognize when I have gone too far. When I am tired, I need rest. When I need help, I ask for it. Sometimes I need help in order to get rest. I may have to take a much needed nap while someone else helps with my loved one or while he is at day care. Other things can wait. If I am not getting the rest I need, I will get sick and that won't help anyone.

Today's Tip: Cut back on the amount of liquids your loved one gets after dinner. This will help if incontinence is a factor. It may also help him sleep through the night without getting up.

MAY 29

When people are in an atmosphere in which they feel safe and secure, they experience a degree of freedom. This enables them to function better. I have that level of comfort when I am with those who support and understand me. I am able to offer a similar atmosphere to my loved one. We all benefit.

Today's Tip: If your loved one won't wear an ID bracelet, consider buying her a good piece of jewelry with the information engraved on it. Have a child or grandchild present it to her if you think that would increase her chances of wearing it. The back of a man's watch can be engraved. Upon finding someone who is confused, most competent authorities will look for identifying information on their jewelry.

MAY 30

I am often mystified by my loved one. He seems to love me and know me one minute and the next he thinks I am someone else. Sometimes he is afraid I am going to harm him. He keeps me on my toes! I expect the unexpected. I'm beginning to understand a not so understandable disease.

Today's Tip: Generally people with dementia work hard at being normal and appropriate in public. However, a low frustration tolerance can accompany dementia. Your loved one may develop a tendency to tell it like it is. You might be able to tactfully stop him from making inappropriate comments by getting his attention and simply putting your finger up to your mouth and shaking your head back and forth — rather like telling a child to hush when someone else is speaking or sleeping.

MAY 31

Life is what happens no matter what we had planned. I'm finally learning every situation is full of opportunities. How I handle what life brings me makes all the difference. My attitude can make me or break me. I don't dwell on life's problems — I dwell on solutions.

Today's Tip: Your loved one may make up stories of how something was stolen or lost. It could be a way of covering up if she fears she is responsible for the disappearance. It's easier to blame someone else. She may also fear being punished. Or, she might actually believe the story. Whatever the reason — listen to her story, show some understanding, and change the subject!

JUNE

JUNE 1

I don't withhold love. I don't withdraw from love. We are all deserving of love and we all need it. I show my love to others. I accept God's love and the love of others. I am learning to love myself. I treat myself with the same love, care, and respect I give others.

Today's Tip: Getting your loved one to operate and wear his seat belt in the car can be a challenge. You may have to do it for him. All the buttons on the inside of the car door can also present problems and confusion. You will eventually find yourself having to help him get in and out. Plan lots of time to get places. The logistics of car rides can be quite time consuming!

JUNE 2

I'm becoming flexible. I am not as rigid as I used to be. There is more than one way to do something. I'm constantly learning new and better ways to accomplish things I've done for years. Sometimes my loved one teaches me, or at times I discover a fresh approach. If there is a more convenient way to get a task done today, we do it the new way!

Today's Tip: When your loved one asks for money, she may be content if you joyfully give her a few dollars and some change to carry in her purse. Trust enough to make her feel secure, but only give a small amount as she may lose it or give it away. Let her have complete control over what you give her.

JUNE 3

There are days when each hour brings changes. Nothing is static. Nothing seems to last for long. So when something good is going on, I enjoy it. If things are a little rough, I don't fret. What happens today probably won't happen tomorrow. Tomorrow will be filled with a newness of its own — I am ready and realistic.

Today's Tip: Be adaptable. If your loved one requires a lot of your attention today, make him your top priority. Everything else is secondary. The house doesn't have to be perfect. Peace and serenity for both of you is your goal.

JUNE 4

I am thankful for small things like being able to sit for five minutes at one time. I celebrate small successes. Little acts of kindness to my loved one seem to make such a big difference. I cherish the beautiful ways she shows her appreciation. A wee laugh or a smile on her face gives me great pleasure.

Today's Tip: One AD car passenger developed the habit of trying to get out of the car every time it stopped at a stoplight. Her caregiver had to refrain from taking her in the car for a while. When transporting her was absolutely necessary, a third party had to ride along to keep her busy and make sure she remained safely within the car.

JUNE 5

Occasionally I catch myself experiencing feelings of resentment. I resent the disruption this disease has caused in our lives. Sometimes I resent what I am called upon to do because of its existence. I realize resentment, like anger, will not do anyone any good. It promotes negative thinking. I have decided to replace it with appreciation. I appreciate my loved one. I appreciate everything I am able to do to help. I find value in what we have.

Today's Tip: Your loved one might resist doing many of the things you ask or need him to do. You may get more cooperation if you ask him to help you. He might feel better thinking he is assisting you. Feeling needed is always nicer than feeling controlled.

JUNE 6

What lies ahead is unclear. It always has been. No one has a crystal ball to predict the future. I have made some necessary financial and legal provisions to make the way smoother for me and my loved one, but I do not dwell on the uncertainty of the future. I never did before. Why should I start now? I take one day at a time — step by step.

Today's Tip: You may have success getting your loved one to relinquish driving by telling him you need more practice. Ask him to help with directions. He may secretly know he shouldn't be driving and you will be giving him a gracious way to stop. Again, he is helping you.

JUNE 7

I don't jump to conclusions. To do so is a form of judgment. I certainly don't want people judging me. So I better not judge them. If a friend lets me down or has a bad day, I try to look behind them for the cause. It is presumptuous to jump to conclusions and take the actions of others personally. I can be understanding.

Today's Tip: Don't impose your way on your loved one unless it is a matter of safety. When it's a matter of safety, be as diplomatic as possible. Try to communicate that she is loved and her safety is important to you.

JUNE 8

I am able and willing to fail. I've learned some of my most valuable lessons from past failures. I am not afraid of trying new things. If I were, I would not have enjoyed any successes. A full life consists of failures and successes. I have a full life.

Today's Tip: Communicate to your loved one that she is still intelligent and capable of many things. She has a valuable self-identity to protect. Discourage any demeaning comments she makes about her own abilities.

JUNE 9

I cannot fix people. I can be here for them. I can be a good listener, a good hand holder, a good friend to a fellow traveler. I cannot travel someone else's journey for them. No matter how close I am to another human being, we have individual paths to walk. God is the only one who can walk the whole way with us.

Today's Tip: Have sandwich meat shaved. It requires less effort to bite and chew.

JUNE 10

Loving is different than liking. I can dislike something someone does and still love the person. I can do things I don't really like to do when I am acting out of love. Love makes all the difference in framing my attitude and actions. I give care out of love.

Today's Tip: If your loved one constantly asks what today's plans are, try posting them each day. When he asks, just point to them. You may want to check things off together when you've done them.

JUNE 11

No human relationship is perfect. No human beings are perfect. I have regrets for some of my past actions. I have regrets for some things I failed to do in the past. I face my regrets and realize they are normal. If I am able to make amends to people, I do so. If not, I share my concerns with a loving God who understands. I can be cleansed of regrets.

Today's Tip: Consider having your largest meal in the middle of the day. It is often easier on the caregiver and the loved one. If sundowning is a factor, this could reduce late afternoon and evening stress for everyone.

JUNE 12

I have overcome many doubts. I doubted a support group would really help my situation. I doubted my abilities as a caregiver. Then, I doubted anyone else could care for my loved one as well as I could. I doubted I could get over every obstacle and when I did I wondered why I doubted. Coming through doubts I have gained strength and faith.

Today's Tip: When dealing with incontinence, take advantage of the numerous baby care products available. Many products help with cleanup. There are lotions, creams, and ointments to keep skin free of infection and rashes. Refrain from referring to incontinence undergarments as diapers. Doing so is degrading.

JUNE 13

I need my energy for positive things. When a negative thought starts to invade my being, I replace it with a positive thought. I won't let negative mental energy rob me of the physical energy caregiving requires. Whenever I'm feeling blue, I call a positive-thinking friend, or I get involved in something that brings me pleasure. I take positive action and do something just for me today.

Today's Tip: Consider exchanging caregiving once or twice a week with another caregiver. As well as providing respite for you, this will give your loved one an opportunity to enjoy doing home activities with a friend. When a day care center or other respite option is not available, this is often a good alternative.

JUNE 14

I no longer push panic buttons. When I remain calm, things are not as bad as they first appear to be. Keeping my calm makes for keeping my head! Everything need not be a crisis or catastrophe. My reactions make a big difference.

Today's Tip: If walking is a problem for your loved one, consider obtaining a handicapped or disabled placard for your car. The regulations and statutes differ from state to state. Applications generally require the signature of your physician and the vehicle owner. It could help make your life a lot easier.

JUNE 15

Part of being a good listener is hearing what concerned family and friends say to me about me. I need to listen when they tell me I look tired or suggest I need a break. When they sincerely express such concerns, I am wise to consider any appropriate help or solutions they offer. If I ignore them they might feel their concerns are not appreciated and I may miss out on some much needed support.

Today's Tip: Many AD groups have formed speakers' bureaus of trained volunteers. They promote understanding and awareness of AD and related disorders to any interested group. You may want to suggest they speak at clubs or organizations you and your loved one are associated with.

JUNE 16

It's important I be emotionally healthy for my loved one's sake — and my own. I do periodic emotional and spiritual checkups on myself. When some feeling or emotion is out of perspective, I have to deal with it. If something like guilt is a persistent factor I advise refraining from unrealistic personal expectations. I prescribe setting realistic goals for myself. Chronic guilt can become crippling if unattended.

Today's Tip: Your loved one may favor certain clothes and insist on wearing them every day. To avoid conflict and constant laundry, purchase duplicates of her favorite outfits — the more the better!

JUNE 17

I cleaned out my inner closet today and found I've been holding onto some inappropriate accessories. They are the masks I sometimes wear. There is the mask of independence that pushes others away. I possess a mask of indifference. One mask portrays that I have no fears. Somehow they don't seem to fit anymore. Through loving support and fellowship with others who care, I am comfortable discarding my masks and uncovering the real me.

Today's Tip: Your loved one's clothes closet and drawers may contain too many items. Remove excess clothing. Some choice is good. It gives him a sense of control. Too many choices can be overwhelming and upset him.

JUNE 18

Humor is a great tool. I use it every day. It helps create a safe friendly environment for my loved one. It provides relief in times of embarrassment. Being slightly ridiculous at times is a great stress reliever for both of us. When we enjoy a good laugh together we both experience a degree of healing.

Today's Tip: Your loved one may be more apt to participate in games if you don't keep score. Just play for the fun of it.

JUNE 19

I've always enjoyed inhabiting a serene setting of my own when I want to relax. It takes a little ingenuity today, but I manage to make time to get there. I maintain a special place where I can curl up with a good book, pick up a favorite hobby, or just feel comfortable.

Today's Tip: We tend to shout or raise our voices when others don't seem to understand or hear what we are saying. Remember to speak your words slowly, calmly, and use the same words if you have to repeat a message to your loved one. If she does not have a hearing problem, keep your voice at a low pitch — loudness and shouting will frighten her.

JUNE 20

The need to feel normal seems to be common among human beings. The first time I shared my feelings at my support group I was relieved to know I was experiencing normal feelings. They understood me when I admitted I felt sorry for myself. They let me cry. They let me grieve over losses. My loved one needs to be understood also. I let him feel. I convey to him that his feelings are normal.

Today's Tip: Use props or cues whenever possible when communicating with your loved one. Go to the door and open it when it is time to leave the room. Say, "It's time for us to go now." This is usually more effective than merely speaking the words alone. The gestures of moving to the door and opening the door can help your communication immensely and may reduce confusion, frustration, and embarrassment for him.

JUNE 21

There is something really special about prayer. Prayer is my connection to God. It comforts and strengthens me. When others tell me they pray for my loved one and me it warms my heart and strengthens my connection with them. What a wonderful bond of love God offers us through prayer.

Today's Tip: If family or friends ask you what you'd like for your birthday, be specific. Tell them if there is something you really want or need. They are asking because they want to get something meaningful for you. If you need something practical like an extra day of day care, now is the opportunity to speak up!

JUNE 22

Touching is essential to human companionship. A hug, a kiss, a reassuring pat can convey feelings of love and acceptance to others. It acknowledges life and connection. May my loved one always feel life and love in my touch!

Today's Tip: If your loved one wanders, you may want to register her in a national database which helps identify and locate lost individuals. Call the National Alzheimer's Association 800 number for information on the Safe Return Program. For a small fee she can be enrolled and receive an ID bracelet or necklace, labels for her clothing, and a wallet ID. The items all carry an 800 number that is operated 24 hours a day. A call to the number begins the search process.

JUNE 23

My efforts may not change things, but I hope they contribute to making a rough way smoother. My goal is to help preserve and maintain a quality of life for someone I love. If I can minimize some pain or suffering, then I am doing enough. If I can make his way a little easier, I will be content.

Today's Tip: When you can't understand something your loved one is saying, respond to his emotional tone. Acknowledge the emotion with compassion. Don't ask what is upsetting him. Be aware of what occurred in the past few moments that might have upset him.

JUNE 24

When I need an answer, it often comes when I least expect it and from a source I don't expect. Sometimes the answer is here all the time and I'm too busy worrying or searching to see it until it is pointed out to me. Often my loved one has a better way of doing things than I do! Her way may take longer than my way, but we usually get it done when we do it her way.

Today's Tip: Limit your relative's intake of coffee and tea. They don't aid in keeping the kidneys flushed like other liquids such as water and juices.

JUNE 25

I'm working on being truthful. When concerned people ask how I'm doing, I don't say I'm feeling fine if it's not the truth. In fact, I'm glad when people ask how I'm doing. It shows they know I am operating in a somewhat unusual arena. Most people just ask how my loved one is. I usually say, "About the same." If they are really interested they'll know we are both affected and ask about both of us at the same time.

Today's Tip: Some of your loved one's childhood language may reappear. Don't be surprised or correct him if he uses childish words for everyday functions or objects. Continue to treat him as an adult, whatever language he chooses to use.

JUNE 26

I am responsible for keeping my loved one safe, well-fed, and clean. I also care about his spiritual well-being. I make sure the things that have always been important to him are still prominent and evident.

Today's Tip: If religious traditions are an important part of your family life, continue to observe them with your loved one. Remember symbols and prayers may still have a strong significance for him. They can be a great source of comfort even if he just partakes quietly.

JUNE 27

"You, too?" I often hear these words
when I share with another caregiver. Usually
they are aired with a sigh of relief that says I'm
not alone. Swapping our experiences and stories
brings solace and companionship.

Today's Tip: Two caregivers developed a
ritual of talking on the phone every night after
their loved ones went to bed. They discussed
their day. They supported each other and found
themselves looking forward to that time together
at the end of each day.

JUNE 28

I feel I must try to stay one step ahead of my loved one. It's not always easy. I get both physically and mentally tired. I must always stay alert. Sometimes she is one step ahead of me! If a mental or physical shortcut is available and works, I don't feel bad about taking it. Whatever works!

Today's Tip: If your loved one locks the bathroom door every time she goes in there, most likely she can't or won't always unlock it. Disable the lock or have new doorknobs installed that don't lock. If the door swings in, have it re-hung to swing out so you can open it easily should she fall while inside the bathroom.

JUNE 29

I don't have to tackle all my problems at once. I need only concentrate on the ones at hand. That's enough! It's too late to solve yesterday's problems. Tomorrow's problems can wait. I'm not even sure what they will be. Only today deserves my attention and energies. Somehow when I am in the middle of working out my daily problems, I cease to view them as problems. They're just a part of the day. They mix in with the good stuff.

Today's Tip: Dressing another adult can be quite a chore. If your loved one is a lady accustomed to panty hose, you may want to opt for knee-high hose instead. Also clothing made of soft, stretchable fabrics that are easy to remove and care for are a must when dealing with incontinence.

JUNE 30

I practice wholesome thinking. It consists of looking for good in others and in myself. It fosters gratitude and joy. It encourages me to dwell on blessings, not misfortunes. I am inspired to see beyond circumstances. Wholesome thinking is healthy thinking.

Today's Tip: Taking the knobs off the stove when you are not using it is a good idea. They can be removed and replaced quickly and easily on most ranges. It's best not to leave your loved one alone in the kitchen when something is cooking.

JULY

JULY 1

I have a new way of reacting to life. I don't force solutions anymore. Force is too controlling. It seldom works and it sets me and those I love up for failure. Calm peaceful solutions are the ones that work. Everyone benefits when a solution is worked out in a comfortable manner for all concerned.

Today's Tip: Stay in touch with the organizations you enjoy, even if you can't attend regularly. If you've been a leader, you might wish to stay involved on a committee that only meets once a month. You may be able to serve as an active member from home on a phone committee. Keep some contact. Don't cancel your memberships.

JULY 2

Help is an interchange. The more I give, the more I get. I've developed a strong awareness of the needs of others. I give more freely. I am more open to those around me — not just to the needs of my loved one. I get the help and serenity I need in return. I'm not always sure where it comes from. It just comes.

Today's Tip: People with dementia often think they are back in their childhood and talk about their parents. One caregiver tried to explain to her loved one his parents were no longer living. He looked so sad and upset. She didn't do it again. Instead, she let him talk about them as much as he wanted. He seemed happier.

JULY 3

I take good care of myself. I make sure my day is as good for me as it is for others. If I need a lift, I do something extra nice for myself. It's important to treat myself as well as I treat others. I am more pleasant to be around when I am well taken care of, too.

Today's Tip: Some caregivers find mealtime easier for their loved one if they present one food at a time. Many items on a plate together can be distracting and confusing. Offering just one utensil also helps. A solid colored plate sets off the food, rather than serving mashed potatoes on a white plate.

JULY 4

Sometimes I just need emotional rest. When my emotions are working overtime I can't get the physical rest I require. I've discovered that some good laughs release the tension and relax me. Reading a humorous book or watching a funny movie often makes me feel lighter and better able to get to sleep.

Today's Tip: Playing catch with a beach ball is a great activity. No one can get hurt and they don't move too fast. Brightly colored beach balls seem to inspire fun and laughter!

JULY 5

I am defined from within. I am called upon to make some choices that are only mine to make. When I am comfortable with myself and my decisions, it doesn't matter if everyone agrees with me or not. My peace has to come from within.

Today's Tip: If hallucinations consist of unfriendly people that frighten or upset your loved one, try being his hero. Open the door and tell the unfriendly people to leave. One caregiver says she just shoos them out whenever they're a problem. Then she quickly suggests she and her loved one enjoy some ice cream!

JULY 6

Caregiving sure gives purpose to my life. In many ways I am living for two. Often I have to interpret my loved one's feelings and needs. Sometimes I am her voice to others. She trusts me to speak for her. She looks to me and I return her concerned look with a nod. I understand.

Today's Tip: Complex instructions are probably not easily understood by your loved one. Always get her attention before you start talking. Make sure she is looking at you and say her name when you begin talking. Give a short message. If you have to repeat a direction, use the exact same words you used the first time. Say the first thing to do, then do it. When it is done, say the next thing. Life goes more smoothly one step at a time. Your loved one will be grateful for your care and patience.

JULY 7

Without challenges I become complacent. Life's challenges stimulate me. I may grumble at times when I feel my life has enough challenges, but they keep me alert and ready. I'm never given something I can't handle. Sometimes my way of handling it is to get help!

Today's Tip: Anger at the disease is normal. Anger directed at your loved one or extreme anger at the disease can seriously affect your caregiving. Your loved one did not cause the disease. She can't control its progression. If you find yourself feeling extremely angry, seek qualified help right away. You will learn ways to appropriately deal with your anger as well as ways to help her deal with the anger she may be experiencing. Inappropriate anger can cause guilt feelings you don't need.

JULY 8

Sometimes truth is too upsetting for my loved one. He cannot internalize an answer that is not acceptable to him. I have learned to say things that work. It is often kinder than reality.

Today's Tip: If your loved one constantly asks what time his sister is coming to visit and you know she isn't coming, you might find it easier to say she is coming tomorrow. He may be more content than if you explain she is not coming because she lives in Europe. You will both be less agitated and he will most likely forget what you said in a few minutes anyway.

JULY 9

I continue to give love whether I see immediate results or not. Love doesn't miss its mark. I know it is being received. I am consistent in giving love. I believe it is the most powerful thing I can do for my loved one and myself.

Today's Tip: If your loved one worries about you while she is at day care, you may consider giving her a reassuring note to carry. Write a simple message addressing her by name. Use short sentences. Tell her where you are, what time you will pick her up, and to stay there until you come. Make sure you tell her you love her and sign your name.

JULY 10

I have relaxed some of my standards. I don't get distraught if the house is not immaculate. Clean and uncluttered is enough. I don't put unreal expectations on myself. I don't push myself. I leave my energy for more important things like helping to make someone's day a little brighter.

Today's Tip: If your loved one does not eat well at meals or has trouble sitting still long enough to eat a good meal, keep nutritious snacks in view all day. Make sure they are snacks that won't spoil and have them where he can see them and get them easily.

JULY 11

Sometimes it is infuriating when I am devoting my time to helping someone who seems to be devoting her time to resisting my help! I remind myself to stop and try to put myself in her shoes. It must be a strange feeling to be dependent on someone's help to do very ordinary things. Resistance is a normal reaction. I will try not to act like I am helping her. I can work on creating an atmosphere of partnership and togetherness. We will help each other get things done.

Today's Tip: Encourage your loved one to dress herself for as long as she can. You may just want to lay her clothes out in the order she will put them on.

JULY 12

No one likes a know-it-all. I'm uncomfortable around someone who has all the answers and never makes mistakes. I prefer human beings. Life is made up of trials and errors. We all make mistakes. Every day I try different things. Some work. Some don't. I am human.

Today's Tip: Make sure your loved one is getting ongoing medical care. He may not be able to use the right vocabulary to describe pain or discomfort. Any sudden unexplainable changes in behavior or bodily functions should be checked out by his physician.

JULY 13

Life is full of compromise. I compromise with my loved one daily, sometimes without her knowledge. We used to compromise by negotiation. Now I prefer to call it adjustment. If she is not in the mood for a shower, we adjust our schedule. We do something else and come back to the shower idea a little later.

Today's Tip: Avoid using patterned tile flooring as it could cause confusion and uneasiness. Your loved one may feel unsure and off-balance walking on it.

JULY 14

I do not have a choice whether to experience pain or not. Life does not come without pain. I don't have control over it. I do have control over whether I choose to suffer or not. I can feel pain without suffering. I feel both the pain and the pleasures of my life. The pains I experience make the pleasures all the richer.

Today's Tip: A glass-top table might be confusing for your loved one at mealtime. Cover the top with a short cloth. Long cloths can get caught in her legs and feet.

JULY 15

I try to maintain interests. I don't have as much time as I'd like for my projects, but I am realistic in the things I choose to undertake. I do things that can be left unattended if I am distracted or needed elsewhere. The projects I enjoy today help relieve stress.

Today's Tip: Portable projects like writing poetry or letters, and any form of needlework or simple crafts are all great stress relievers for caregivers. They can be left easily and picked up again at anytime.

JULY 16

Each day I become more confident in my role as a caregiver. I am somehow comforted knowing I am comforting another. I am making a difference in someone else's life. I am learning to make wise choices and decisions for both me and my loved one. I get better at it day by day, step by step.

Today's Tip: If the toilet and the floor are the same color, you may have to make some adjustments to differentiate between them. An easy solution is a bathroom rug of a different color. Use the type that is cut out to go around the base of the toilet. It also helps if the wall behind the toilet is a different color than the toilet. Do anything to make the toilet stand out.

JULY 17

Not only do I break my loved one's tasks down step by step, I break my own tasks down step by step. I don't let either one of us get overwhelmed. It's as important to keep my stress level down as it is his. I don't overburden myself. We both take it easy. We do what we can.

Today's Tip: Putting bells on doors might help make your life easier. Bells on the bedroom door can signal you if your loved one gets up during the night. Bells on outside doors help if he is a wanderer and a master at opening locked doors.

JULY 18

I concentrate on my loved one, not on the disease. My focus is on her care. My attention to the disease is positive, not negative. I keep informed on new developments and research being done. I support all the efforts to find a cure and prevention. I help others understand and care.

Today's Tip: Big is not always better. Large rooms, large crowds, large television sets can present problems for some dementia patients.

JULY 19

Nothing is worth getting everyone upset, including myself. My reactions to things make a big difference to me and my loved one. I am in the driver's seat when it comes to setting the tone of our day. If I act like some task is a big deal and of utmost importance I make the mood tense for everyone. My new motto is "Don't make anything a big deal!"

Today's Tip: Serve foods at room temperature -- nothing too hot or too cold.

JULY 20

Relinquishing my self-will is sometimes difficult for me to do. I've always been in charge and in control. I am learning an important thing. I must let go of what I cannot control. I am not in charge of everything in my life. I can't will certain things to be. I must trust God and release my hold on the things only he can control.

Today's Tip: It may become increasingly difficult for your loved one to screen out distractions. Before speaking to her, try to eliminate other noises or activities that might make it hard for her to give you her attention. Be attentive yourself to the things that seem to distract or cause her agitation.

JULY 21

My journal serves another purpose in my life. In referring back to it, I discover it is not only good therapy. It is also a log in which I am able to identify patterns. In it I find clues to being a better caregiver. It contains the problems we encounter surrounded by important information such as how often a certain behavior occurs, what events take place that might trigger the behavior, and what solutions work and what doesn't help. I congratulate myself on the discipline of keeping a journal.

Today's Tip: Don't put your loved one on the spot. Anticipate and avoid situations that could be embarrassing for him.

JULY 22

The most valuable gift I can give my loved one is love. Things can loose their value and function. Things can't be taken everywhere we go. Love can still be felt when we lose the ability to feel or comprehend other things. Love somehow gets through to the human spirit. Perhaps because it is essential to the human spirit.

Today's Tip: You don't have to entertain your loved one. Keep boredom for both of you at a minimum, but don't wear yourself out trying to create things to do. A pleasant comfortable atmosphere is important.

JULY 23

Simple inexpensive activities can bring me pleasure. Some days I need to set aside my normal routine and do something refreshing. A walk in the park, purchasing a frivolous magazine, a trip to the zoo, or a matinee movie are affordable and invigorating.

Today's Tip: Get in the habit of using short sentences. Give your loved one time to interpret what you say. Don't string a lot of sentences together. Chances are she can only remember a few words at a time.

JULY 24

Music has magical qualities. I've always enjoyed music, but now I see a value in it I never realized before. It can be soothing and calming to the human spirit. It is a mood setter. It can be a peacemaker. A spontaneous waltz with my loved one works miracles. An impromptu sing-a-long chases away cares and frustrations. Music has found a special place in my heart.

Today's Tip: Music can be used to encourage exercise. Select appropriate background music for the exercises or activities your relative engages in. Routine mild exercise is extremely important. Using the same familiar music each time can be reassuring, encouraging, and serve as a helpful cue to movements.

JULY 25

My patience is tested a lot. Sometimes I lose it! I'm getting better at forgiving myself when I do lose my patience. I'm even learning to forgive myself quickly and go on. I remind myself the moment won't be remembered in a minute or two by my loved one. I am being hard on myself if I keep reliving it.

Today's Tip: Some caregivers discourage nocturnal trips to the kitchen. They put a favorite snack on the bedside table after their loved one has gone to sleep.

JULY 26

My loved one may be childlike in some of her behavior. Her reactions to the world around her are often those of a child. She is childlike, but not teachable. It is I who must learn for both of us. I must learn new ways of nurturing and enjoying our relationship.

Today's Tip: Give your loved one unimportant mail to open. It may prove important to her. It can be a useful activity for her while you attend to other mail or activities.

JULY 27

I have made many wise investments in my life. Now I am investing my time and energy into helping another human being through a difficult time in her life. It is probably the most important and worthwhile investment I have ever made.

Today's Tip: When considering in-home health care, check out all the pros and cons between going through an agency or hiring someone privately. For instance, an agency usually handles all the necessary payroll taxes and workman's compensation insurance. If you choose to hire someone privately you may be responsible.

JULY 28

I explore every avenue, nook and cranny for assistance in caregiving. I take advantage of all physical, emotional, educational and financial resources available to me. I treat caregiving with as much respect as any vocation I have ever undertaken. It is serious business. It is as deserving of the best attention and up-to-date technologies as any other calling.

Today's Tip: Although your loved one may have given up driving, he might still be able to ride a bike. Riding together is great exercise. It can be a way of keeping in touch with the neighbors and the neighborhood.

JULY 29

When I am confused about something, I do a few things to see my way through the uncertainty. First, I ask God for direction. I have to trust that he hears me. Then I quiet myself so I can hear him. I clear my head so I can relax. When I am truly quiet and calm inside, he helps me see things more clearly.

Today's Tip: A small blackboard is ideal for writing or posting daily messages. Try it for posting answers to the latest most frequently asked questions.

JULY 30

I am gaining greater insight into my self —
my strengths and weaknesses. My strengths are
stronger and different. Some of my old strengths
are not appropriate any more. Oddly, some of
the things I considered weak, like gentleness and
tenderness, are the strengths that get me through
each day.

Today's Tip: For restaurant dining you may
wish to prepare a little card in advance to
discretely hand your waiter. Write a short
message explaining your companion has a
memory problem and you would like any
questions regarding the menu choice directed to
you. Thank the waiter for his patience and
understanding.

JULY 31

Accepting that something can be gained from every experience is inspiring. Each encounter is unique and this moment will happen only once. The old saying to make the best of each minute is upbeat and makes a great deal of sense. I will look for the good in each moment and live it up!

Today's Tip: Although your loved one might still be able to shower or bathe alone, you may feel the need to monitor the process without intruding on his privacy. Suggest leaving the door ajar a bit to let the steam out. You will be better able to check how well the bathing process is going without appearing nosy.

AUGUST

AUGUST 1

I know my loved one's heart. That cannot change. The heart keeps the beautiful things safe. His outer world may be getting smaller and he cannot always express what's in his heart, but I know how big and splendid his heart really is. I smile and gently squeeze his hand. He knows I know.

Today's Tip: Some communities have formed social groups for caregiving spouses. It's an opportunity for caregivers to participate in activities like attending plays, sports, or pot-luck dinners. If you are caring for a spouse, get a reliable person to take over once in a while so you can enjoy these social events.

AUGUST 2

It is not within my power to impose my ways and coping methods on another individual. When I hear someone share a situation similar to some of mine, I am tempted to tell them what to do. Instead, I relate that I experience the same problem. If they ask, I simply share what works for me. I really don't know if it will work for them.

Today's Tip: Watch your loved one's body language. If a situation becomes combative, stop and back up. We cannot control another person no matter how close we are. We can, however, change the activity. Offer a favorite food or suggest a dance or a hug as a pleasant distraction.

AUGUST 3

I must be honest with myself regarding my behavior. I am experiencing some trying times. If I am using sarcasm when talking to others, I may be covering up some resentments or envy. Am I feeling a little sorry for myself? It would be better to admit my feelings for what they are. They are mine and I am entitled to them. I am not entitled to abuse others with sarcasm or nasty remarks.

Today's Tip: If your loved one is fearful of having a shampoo in the shower, doing it at the sink or going to the beauty parlor may work. You might want to consider a dry shampoo for a while.

AUGUST 4

I am learning to simplify my life. I am better able to focus my attention on the things that really matter. The simplicity has a spiritual effect on me. I am more at peace. My life has new direction and meaning.

Today's Tip: It's better not to talk about tomorrow's plans ahead of time. Wait until right before you do an activity. This is less confusing for your loved one and helps you remain flexible.

AUGUST 5

My work is never done and neither am I. I am still in the process of becoming me. I realize it is a long on-going process. I do not rush with the things I have to do and I do not rush with my own progress. I allow myself time. I treat myself with the same patience I do others.

Today's Tip: A sturdy rocking chair may be the answer for an anxious or fidgety loved one. Rocking might prove to be a good alternative to pacing.

AUGUST 6

Prevention has become an important aspect of my life. One of my prime roles is safety officer. I am constantly aware of safety. I guard against potential hazards in our home. I am also aware of possible disturbing emotional situations. I try to prevent them from happening. I stay alert.

Today's Tip: Give your home periodic and thorough safety checks. Keep in mind your loved one's current level of dementia and safety-proof accordingly. All prescriptions and over-the-counter medications should be locked in a safe place. Sharp objects may have to be put away, electric appliances monitored or hidden, windows locked — do whatever it takes to help insure safety.

AUGUST 7

My words and messages need to be direct, not offensive. In the past, I have not always been tactful and the responses were not always desirable. Now I choose my words carefully, anticipating the effect they may have on my loved one. It is considerate. Diplomacy is appropriate.

Today's Tip: Your loved one may not recognize when he is thirsty. Water is the most important liquid for him. Soda, coffee, tea, and some juices can be strong and don't take the place of water. Diluting these beverages can be a good idea — but make sure he drinks plenty of plain water every day.

AUGUST 8

Today doesn't come with a map or directions. I am free to choose my way through the day. I can take a winding dirt road full of potholes and puddles or I can get on a smooth straight path. They will both get me to the end of the day. It's up to me what route I take.

Today's Tip: You might want to remove all credit cards from your loved one's wallet or purse. If hiding and losing items is a problem, try to substitute good jewelry with inexpensive jewelry.

AUGUST 9

Life does not come without disappointments. It also does not come without satisfactions. If it weren't for the disappointments I would not have the proper respect for or recognize the satisfactions. There is value in both. A full life could not exist without them.

Today's Tip: Daily teeth brushing can become a problem for your loved one. Encourage her by modeling as you brush your teeth. Early in the disease have her teeth cleaned and checked. Continue routine appointments if possible for prevention. Sometimes a children's dentist has more patience with uncooperative adults. Maintaining good oral hygiene is difficult, but necessary. Familiarize yourself with such helpful products as disposable sponge toothbrushes, fluoridated mouthwash rinse, and edible toothpaste.

AUGUST 10

My loved one and I perform a lot of tasks together. We're good co-workers. We stop and take breaks often. We reward ourselves when we have done a job well. We may sit and admire our work or go outside for a breath of fresh air. We eat good snacks while on breaks. This is a great place to work!

Today's Tip: It's a good idea for your loved one to go to the bathroom right before going to bed and before every meal.

AUGUST 11

I've been reintroduced to the wonderful world of make believe. My loved one and I often discuss frivolous things. We can both be creative and imaginative. The discussions and laughter are light and joyful. Sometimes we talk about a color or a butterfly. The exchange is fascinating. It's fun for both of us.

Today's Tip: Some nursery schools and adult day care programs have found the value in getting together once in a while. The interaction between the children and the adults is usually very positive.

AUGUST 12

I'm entitled to a bonus — something unusual that I don't expect. Let's see, what can I surprise myself with? A professional manicure and pedicure? A day off? A round of golf? What would truly delight me? I deserve a treat today! I'm worth it!

Today's Tip: You may find you have to remind your loved one to chew food thoroughly. He could be confused as to when to chew and when to swallow. Try demonstrating for him or tell him when to chew and when to swallow. Make sure meals are not rushed or tense.

AUGUST 13

My days are sprinkled with large doses of common sense. When I apply common sense to most things I encounter, the days run more smoothly. I don't have to be a rocket scientist to know the right formula. Good old-fashioned common sense mixed well with equally large doses of love and compassion are the main ingredients that make up my days.

Today's Tip: Agree, agree, agree. If agreeing with your loved one keeps peace and does not endanger her safety, don't rock the boat by having to be right. She might be content doing an activity that makes no sense to you at all. If it's harmless and doesn't present a real problem for you, let her do it.

AUGUST 14

I find I must allow for some amount of independence for my loved one within the realm of safety. I also require a degree of independence. There are some activities and tasks he can perform relatively unsupervised. Knowledge of his abilities, behavior, and attention span permits me to take some calculated risks.

Today's Tip: Closing all drapes and blinds at nighttime could help with sundowning. Keep the rooms well lit but not glaring. It might help to do whatever you can to make the atmosphere in your home seem like daytime.

AUGUST 15

I don't knock myself out, but I do what I can to create a pleasing environment for my loved one. I also benefit when a calmness permeates the air. I want the mood to be warm and friendly for all. There is an atmosphere of love and peace in our home. The sun shines into our home and our hearts.

Today's Tip: Be aware that changes in your loved one's way of life and surroundings can cause changes in his behavior. You cannot avoid or stop all the changes that occur around your loved one.

AUGUST 16

I don't push others. So why do I push myself? I should give myself the same considerations I give others. It seems egotistical to expect more from myself than I do from others. I need to give myself some slack. I need to relax. I need to get off my own back!

Today's Tip: If your loved one wears dentures, you will have to monitor their care. You may also have to monitor their location when not in her mouth. Some dementia patients misplace them, throw them out, or flush them down the toilet.

AUGUST 17

I am getting better at remaining calm in the midst of confusion. Sometimes I feel as confused with my loved one as she is with the world around her. If I appear confused, I cannot help her. She relies on me for stability. My composure is a foundation for her. I want to provide strong support when she needs it most.

Today's Tip: Upstairs bedrooms present some serious safety problems for loved ones who wander around at night or get up unnoticed. Gates across the top of the stairway and locks on windows are probably in order. A hook and eye lock on the outside of her bedroom door may be necessary to keep her in her room when she goes to bed.

AUGUST 18

When I carry something around for a long time it gets heavier. Carrying it for too long becomes uncomfortable. Sometimes someone will offer to help me carry it. It would be silly to turn down their offer. Sharing makes it lighter. What I am carrying may be a hidden feeling I need to share. It may be a precious package I am carrying. I need assistance if it becomes too much for me to carry alone. Whatever it is, two of us may do a better job handling it together.

Today's Tip: The care your loved one receives while attending a day care facility can differ from in-home care. Day care provides a secure environment with trained staff. Activities and socialization are part of the day. Some in-home care individuals may only sit with your loved one. Check out all the possibilities and choose what is best for your situation.

AUGUST 19

Grief and sorrow can be caused by numerous things. Losses of many kinds can bring on grief. Sometimes grief comes before closure. It is not always good-bye. It can be many little good-byes. I grieve a little every day at the losses I observe. Understanding why I feel this ongoing grief helps me deal with it in realistic manageable ways.

Today's Tip: It is natural for you to be experiencing some feelings of grief when you are daily observing progressive dementia in someone you love. Allowing yourself to acknowledge and feel this emotion is healthy. It isn't good to suppress it. You may want to discuss what you are feeling with other caregivers, your clergy, a close family member, or a professional counselor.

AUGUST 20

My caregiving responsibilities change often to meet the ever-changing demands of progressive dementia. I constantly seek new knowledge. Fresh sources of information and resources are necessary. I realize different stages of AD require different levels of care. I want the best care for my loved one at every stage.

Today's Tip: Even if you plan to always care for your loved one at home, it is wise to learn about the nursing homes in your community. You never know exactly what the future will bring. Investigating and creating a contingency plan while you are not in a crisis situation makes good sense. Just getting on a waiting list does not in any way commit you. Without advance planning your choices could be limited.

AUGUST 21

I have overcome a lot of things. I have overcome my fear of the dementia itself. I am no longer afraid to be a caregiver. I will give the best care I am capable of giving. I am no longer hesitant to ask for help when I need it. I am not bashful about making sure my needs are met along with those of my loved one.

Today's Tip: Even if your loved one hasn't shown a tendency to wander or get lost, it's a good idea to keep a recent close-up photo and a full-length photo of him on hand.

AUGUST 22

I like compliments, so I never miss the opportunity to compliment someone else. One compliment can go a long way on a hard day. When you receive a compliment you see yourself in a better way – the way others see you. A compliment can point out something you never before appreciated about yourself. Giving and receiving compliments should be a required part of everyone's day!

Today's Tip: Large plastic traffic signs can be purchased in some stores. Stop signs and arrows hung on walls are often effective in directing AD loved ones.

AUGUST 23

My loved one is the only star in her own play. She resists all my help. She wants no direction and no supporting cast. At times I let her have the stage. Other times I have to step in and up-stage her for her own good.

Today's Tip: Some AD loved ones have been known to eat plants. It's wise to know which ones are harmful. Remove poisonous plants from the house.

AUGUST 24

My loved one has become a non-conformist. At times I find his somewhat odd behavior amusing. This enlightenment comes to me usually after the fact, however. When I think of some of his rather bizarre behavior, I realize if it is not harming him or anyone else, it can be refreshing. I try to spare him any embarrassment and at the same time let him be a free spirit.

Today's Tip: A flat damp dishcloth placed under your loved one's dinner plate will prevent it from sliding. Or, marine and camper supply stores sell excellent non-slip materials which can be placed under plates and glasses.

AUGUST 25

There is a definite difference between being lonely and being alone. Sometimes I need to be alone. I am never lonely at those times. At other times I can be lonely in a crowd of people. There are times I feel both alone and lonely. When I need the company of others, I reach out. I call someone. I make plans.

Today's Tip: Sometimes your loved one also needs the companionship and stimulation of other people. If appropriate, invite family or friends over for frequent visits. Don't forget the companionship she can find at day care. Neither one of you should be deprived of social contacts.

AUGUST 26

Sometimes when I don't know what to do I find it is best to do nothing. If I take some time before acting or making a decision, I am usually more comfortable and confident. This is not always possible in an emergency situation. But, even pausing a few seconds to clear my thought process and asking God for guidance helps during an immediate crisis.

Today's Tip: Familiarize yourself with a toy shop. Plastic tools, talking dolls, and numerous other items could prove fascinating and enjoyable for your loved one.

AUGUST 27

Balance is a factor in almost every aspect of my life. If I concentrate too much on any one thing, it gets out of balance and so do I. When I am self-centered and concentrate on myself and not on others, I am out of balance. Conversely, I cannot put all of my attention on others and neglect my needs. Life is a broad spectrum. Balance is essential.

Today's Tip: When leaving your loved one in the care of another person or at day care, make sure you advise them of any unusual words or terms he uses to express his needs or concerns. Tell the interim caregiver the words your loved one uses to communicate the need to use the bathroom. Tell the person the words you use to comfort and reassure your loved one.

AUGUST 28

Today I am going to put my cares on the shelf and not think about them. I need a mental break. I can take a mental vacation. Only I know the right atmosphere needed to do this. I will seek out that atmosphere and breathe lighter today.

Today's Tip: Look in the phone book and circle all the restaurants that deliver. When you need a breather, call one of them. Consider choosing an ethnic cuisine. Set the table and atmosphere accordingly. Play appropriate music on the stereo. Enjoy!

AUGUST 29

Stretching is supposed to be good exercise. I believe I am stretching all the time. I've become very good at stretching. I stretch my abilities to meet ever-changing demands. I stretch the finances to meet all our needs. Most importantly, I stretch my arms out to hug my loved one.

Today's Tip: Touching and fingering textures and fabrics can help soothe agitation. Be creative. Make some swatches of different fibers, weaves, and surfaces for your loved one to stroke and feel.

If some objects cause confusion or agitation for my loved one and they are not essential items, I put them out of sight. Perhaps they agitate her because she knows they are familiar and she struggles too hard trying to remember or find the place for them in her memory.

Today's Tip: Keep a fidgeter busy. String some common everyday items together on a short cord and knot the end. Use an empty spool of thread, plastic spoons or measuring cups with holes in them, or any safe objects you think might keep her attention for a while.

AUGUST 31

When I am tempted to worry about tomorrow, I remind myself that tomorrow is more likely to run smoothly if I manage things well today. This makes it even more imperative that I take one day at a time. I will live in today and take care of it.

Today's Tip: Fire departments provide stickers for windows to identify bedrooms of children and handicapped individuals. You might want to put one on your loved one's bedroom window.

SEPTEMBER

SEPTEMBER 1

I cannot work out someone else's difficulties for them. This is particularly hard to accept when a loved one is struggling. I can offer support. I can give reassurance that I am here with them. I cannot carry all their burdens for them, even though I would like to.

Today's Tip: Home security system companies specialize in keeping people out. They may also be helpful at keeping someone in. If wandering or night walking are a problem, explain your situation to an experienced alarm company. They may suggest door alarms, pressure sensitive mats to go under carpet, infra-red detectors, or other devices to help make your life easier.

SEPTEMBER 2

The life I now pattern for myself helps keep me from feeling swamped. I don't try to do more than I can handle at one time. If everything on my list doesn't get done, so what? Peace and serenity are more important to me than setting records.

Today's Tip: A caregiver told of how her relative found lemon oil in the cleaning closet. She poured it on food thinking it was salad dressing. Don't assume because something is not in the kitchen, that it won't find it's way there!

SEPTEMBER 3

The old me would have been overwhelmed by some of the days I have experienced lately. Now I am not as easily discouraged. I know there are good days and there are not so good days. I can handle both kinds.

Today's Tip: It is a lot easier to be honest and free to discuss what you are experiencing with all your family. After all, the whole family is affected by anything that happens to one of its members. There are excellent books available for children and teens explaining AD in a loving way they can understand and relate to.

SEPTEMBER 4

The only decisions I can make are the ones I am able to live with comfortably. The minute I make a decision I am uncomfortable with I know I made the wrong decision. I am free to change my decision. Sometimes I make a decision I am comfortable with at the time and then things beyond my control change. It is within my control to change my mind again and make a new more appropriate decision.

Today's Tip: Wincing when chewing, tenderness when someone touches his mouth or side of his face, and bad breath could indicate a tooth or gum problem in your loved one.

SEPTEMBER 5

If I feel I am doing it all and doing it all alone, I need to ask myself some very important questions. Have I shut out people who have offered to help? Do I take advantage of the support and respite opportunities my community offers? Do I know what my community offers? It may be time to swallow my pride and get some help with this awesome responsibility.

Today's Tip: A telephone answering machine can have many advantages. Keep it on even when you are at home. You don't have to answer if you are busy. Take and return calls when it is convenient for you. This can be a great stress reliever. It is also a safety factor when you are engaged in an activity with your loved one which he cannot do unattended.

SEPTEMBER 6

After a smooth flowing day, besides rejoicing, I try to think about the factors that contributed to the success of the day. Is there anything I can do to perpetuate those factors again? I realize things just seem to flow some days and other days are filled with obstacles. But, when I can see a pattern or determine the best time of day for certain activities I try to utilize this information. I'll take advantage of anything I can do to help us experience more days that run smoothly!

Today's Tip: It's best to have the food prepared and ready to serve before you ask your loved one to sit down to eat.

SEPTEMBER 7

Stepping into any unfamiliar territory is frightening. My loved one and I are both stepping into our own individual unknown territories. I am relatively new at caregiving and it seems to change every day. She is walking into her own new uncharted territory filled with change. We are moving into different unknowns together. Perhaps by holding hands we can support one another and both of us will walk less tentatively.

Today's Tip: Accompany your words with hand motions. When you ask your loved one to join you in an activity, motion with your hands at the same time.

SEPTEMBER 8

Nature has a way of diverting me from my cares. Fresh air, birds, trees, flowers, and the ocean are all beautiful ways God gives me refreshment. When I take time to enjoy nature, I walk lighter and smile more. A gentleness overtakes me. I feel God's loving arms around me when I am surrounded with his magnificent creation.

Today's Tip: Bird feeders and bird baths provide wonderful peaceful entertainment.

SEPTEMBER 9

I must not expect appreciation. Many of my efforts are met with resistance. Not only does resistance come from my loved one, sometimes it comes from other family members. Relationships often become strained when we share a common stress. Some of the stress comes when we don't share the cares and responsibilities. Appreciation of my own personal efforts must come from within myself.

Today's Tip: A foot bath can provide relaxation for you and your loved one.

SEPTEMBER 10

One of the best suggestions I heard through my AD support group was to begin using respite services in the early days of caregiving. When respite is planned on a regular routine schedule early on, caregiver burnout is less likely to occur. When a caregiver keeps stress at a manageable level by making time for respite, the longer the loved one can be cared for at home.

Today's Tip: In older people dry skin is more apt to be a problem than oily skin. After bathing, pat the skin dry rather than rubbing. Avoid the use of body powders. For obvious safety reasons don't use bath oil in the tub or shower.

SEPTEMBER 11

I realize I have my own forms of resistance. When I struggle I am actually resisting. Struggling keeps me from working through a problem. I am too busy constructing my own mental road blocks. When I give up struggling, I am open to learning. I can see my way through road blocks. I can work my way to solutions.

Today's Tip: A raised toilet device and grab bars installed on the walls next to the toilet will make getting on and off easier for your loved one.

SEPTEMBER 12

I need a little space — a little separateness. Sometimes a few minutes is all I need. I am creative in finding ways to keep my loved one occupied and safe while I breathe alone for a while. I try to understand what he is going through. I realize I represent security to him. He worries about me when he cannot see me. I will do all I can to reassure him and at the same time make time for me to be me.

Today's Tip: If your loved one refuses to go to bed, don't fight it. It might be easier to let him sleep wherever he wants to. Maybe a certain chair or sofa feels more comfortable to him right now.

SEPTEMBER 13

In dealing with my loved one's memory loss, I have to readjust my expectations often. Something she was able to remember yesterday, she may not be able to remember today. A direction she followed yesterday may prove to be impossible for her to understand today. Not only do I readjust my expectations, I have learned to increase my patience, my understanding, and my tolerance level.

Today's Tip: When your loved one seems to forget names and faces, you might want to print the names of family members under their pictures and display them. See if this helps. If it proves to increase her frustrations, remove them.

SEPTEMBER 14

I don't make my loved one live in the present like I do. The past has become more familiar to him. No matter what I do, it is not possible for me to keep him in the present. He is more comfortable in the past. Part of adapting my relationship with him is enjoying any old memories we can share. If I do not relate to the times or memories, I can listen and I might even learn some great family history!

Today's Tip: Keep hair dryers, electric shavers, and all electrical appliances away from the bathroom sink or any other source of water.

SEPTEMBER 15

Difficult times in life often bring out unrecognized strengths. I have experienced this in myself. I can see it in others. My loved one may be losing some of her abilities, but she also exhibits many strengths and much courage. I observe the strength of fellow caregivers at our support group. We all help each other when added strength is needed. Sometimes the emotional strength I see in others is all I need to boost mine.

Today's Tip: You can buy special bath or shower chairs that have holes in them for the water to drain through.

SEPTEMBER 16

I am not an expert on caregiving so I don't have all the answers. I am not rigid. I consider the advice of others. I don't turn a deaf ear. I am open to all possibilities and options. I try different ways of doing things to determine what is best for me and my loved one.

Today's Tip: Male caregivers — don't be bashful about asking for help with mending if sewing is not one of your attributes. If you don't have a close friend or family member who might do it, look in the phone book. Or, ask your dry cleaner if he can suggest someone.

SEPTEMBER 17

Whatever my loved one takes seriously, I try to take seriously — even when I don't see the logic in it. What is important is the compassion I show. It will go a lot further than disagreeing with him. I won't rain on his parade.

Today's Tip: Care of fingernails and toenails are an important part of personal hygiene. Nail trimming is easier after a warm shower, bath or foot bath. The nails won't be as hard to trim and your loved one may be more relaxed after bathing. If your loved one is a female, she may enjoy having her nails painted. A professional manicure or assistance in this area by another family member might be a fun treat for her. Having it done on a regular basis could provide respite time for you.

SEPTEMBER 18

I am careful in my communication with my loved one. I don't split hairs. I try not to make anything a big deal. It isn't worth it in the long run. I cannot compete with her or worry about making my point when logic is no longer a factor in our discussions. If I want to engage in debates, I must do so with others.

Today's Tip: Your loved one doesn't need to be corrected — just accepted.

SEPTEMBER 19

I know when to stop. If my loved one and I begin a task together and it is obvious he does not want to do it or it is frustrating him, we stop and do something else. We can come back to the project at a better time. He can't be pushed. If I do push, we both get upset and frustrated. I know when an activity is going nowhere fast. I'm even getting better at recognizing when not to start certain activities. Timing is important.

Today's Tip: If something is lost, learn to look first in your loved one's favorite hiding places. He won't recall hiding them, but you can save yourself time by knowing where missing items are most likely to be found.

SEPTEMBER 20

I can be organized and thorough in my caregiving, but I must have a certain amount of flexibility. Striving for and insisting on perfection in myself or my loved one is unrealistic. I give myself permission to relax and leave a few *I's* not dotted and a few *T's* not crossed.

Today's Tip: One caregiver was having an awful time finding the right time for his loved one's bath. She resisted bathing during the day or evening. The caregiver discovered that his relative was really protesting undressing and then dressing. She was agreeable to bathing right after she got up in the morning. Then, she'd get dressed for the day!

SEPTEMBER 21

It's good to take a personal inventory every once in awhile to see how caregiving is affecting me. Am I getting enough sleep? Am I eating too much, or too little? Am I abusing any drugs, alcohol, or medications? Am I taking my frustrations out on other family members? If I see any destructive patterns emerging, I must find constructive ways to minimize the stress factors. Better coping methods, more respite, and additional help with caregiving may all be in order.

Today's Tip: You are not alone. Call the closest AD helpline number or your local agency on aging. They can lead you to social workers who can assess your needs and help create a good respite plan so you can stay healthy.

SEPTEMBER 22

I don't like to control others or be controlled by others. In the role of caregiver I have to direct my loved one and protect her from harm. She is not always able to control her actions or behavior. She looks to me for help. In caregiving I am often called upon to bring about desired results. I can do this with gentleness and kindness — without appearing controlling.

Today's Tip: Herbal teas contain no caffeine and can be very calming and soothing. Warm milk can have the same effect.

SEPTEMBER 23

I never tell my loved one to try harder. I know he is doing his best. I encourage him and praise him. Positive reinforcements go much further than negative comments. People just naturally keep trying when they are praised and encouraged. Criticism causes discouragement. I will do all I can to cheer him. I'm a great cheerleader!

Today's Tip: A backrub or massage right before bedtime can help relax your loved one and encourage sleep. It might be something he enjoys and provides an incentive to going to bed when it is time.

SEPTEMBER 24

Paying attention to my loved one's physical comfort is as important as his emotional comfort. He is not always able to convey pain or discomfort. I have become aware of behaviors, facial expressions, and body language that communicate his discomfort. If he says he is cold or is shivering even though I am hot, I know his brain is telling him he is cold and he believes it. I understand and get him a sweater.

Today's Tip: Monitor the use of condiments such as salt and pepper. Your loved one may use them repeatedly, not remembering he just used them.

SEPTEMBER 25

I am learning a lot about myself through writing and reading my journal. It not only helps me in caregiving, it helps me view my personal growth. It is a healthy way to express the strong emotions and feelings I have. It is private and comforting. My journal has become a trusted friend.

Today's Tip: If your loved one insists on smoking, you should discretely supervise the activity.

SEPTEMBER 26

I can be angry at the disease and with the circumstances. I can do nothing about the disease at this time. I can try to improve the circumstances. It is inappropriate to vent any anger at my loved one, at myself, or others. To do so would be unproductive and cause me guilt and further anxiety. I will direct all my energies into positive actions.

Today's Tip: One creative caregiver made use of her loved one's repetitive actions and desire to pace. She discovered he loved running the electric sweeper. He was busy, he was helping, and the exercise seemed to help him sleep better at night.

SEPTEMBER 27

The decisions I make are not sudden reactions to crisis situations. Some crises may be turning points and require decision-making, but I try to approach the decision-making process calmly. I consider all the options. I use all the knowledge and tools at my disposal. When appropriate and available, I welcome discussion with other family members. As the primary caregiver, I retain the right to make decisions.

Today's Tip: Hand puppets can be fun and comforting. They help encourage conversation and laughter. They can be purchased at toy stores or, if you feel creative, make some out of socks!

SEPTEMBER 28

I encourage mobility in my loved one and me. We both benefit from regular exercise. I adjust the type of exercise to changes in her and to the season. Whenever possible we get plenty of fresh air. It's good for our mental outlook to get out and walk or go for a ride.

Today's Tip: Never leave your loved one alone in the car — not even for a minute.

SEPTEMBER 29

My loved one's emotions are not lost. I need to remind family and friends of this fact. He feels left out when he is not included in conversation. People tend to talk to him through me lately. This is upsetting to me and my loved one. People are not deliberately uncaring. They just don't understand. I have to help others be aware of our feelings.

Today's Tip: All firearms should be removed from your home. Memory impaired people are liable to mistake a family member for an intruder. If selling the firearms or giving them to other family members is not an option, consider placing the unloaded guns in a large bank safety deposit box.

SEPTEMBER 30

I can't expect friends to automatically reach out to help. They have no idea just how our life is changing. They are unsure about intruding or making a mistake. If I want their help, I must communicate to them my understanding of the dementia process. I need to tell them I am learning day by day. I make plenty of mistakes. I can use the support of close friends who care.

Today's Tip: Consider having your loved one's car keys re-notched without his knowledge. Put them back on his key ring. They won't work in the ignition and maybe he'll just give up trying.

OCTOBER

OCTOBER 1

I never know when my loved one will decide to do something illogical or dangerous. I must keep a fairly constant vigilance over her. This is sometimes difficult because she seems to feel I am always watching her. Often she appears suspicious of my intentions. I want her to feel like an adult, and yet, I need to know she is safe. I'm getting good at acting nonchalant and disguising my watch over her.

Today's Tip: Try using sturdy stable mugs for beverages rather than cups and glasses.

OCTOBER 2

I try not to find fault with my loved one. If I cannot overlook her mistakes, I try to make a joke and find humor in them. I never laugh at her. I cherish her and do not want to hurt her feelings in any way. I try to boost her up, not tear her down. I am very careful with her spirit.

Today's Tip: Nouns are usually the first words a memory impaired person loses. Some caregivers make loose-leaf books with pictures of familiar things like a car, food, a tree, a cat, and so on. When the loved one has trouble finding a word in conversation, the caregiver flips through the book and helps find the picture of the word they are looking for.

OCTOBER 3

My loved one is used to be being recognized and appreciated. I am aware that this need still exists. I use his name whenever I speak to him. I make a point of appreciating the things he does. He seems to know when he does not do something well. I encourage him to do the things he can do well. I want him to continue to enjoy the sense of accomplishment he is accustomed to.

Today's Tip: A sense of helping others and feeling needed is still important to your loved one. You'll find it much easier to gain his cooperation and participation in activities if he feels useful.

OCTOBER 4

Isolation can become a habit. It is a habit I must avoid. Isolation is not good for me or my loved one. We both need the company of others. Sometimes he may object to going to day care or to having someone in. Sometimes I am tired and figure it is easier to stay home than go to a meeting or social engagement. These are often the times we need the stimulation of others the most. Too much isolation can become depressing. We both need uplifting, not the monotony of isolation.

Today's Tip: If your loved one has trouble following the plots of stories or dramas on television, perhaps nature series or musical programs that don't require concentration are more in order.

OCTOBER 5

I am winning battles with myself, not my loved one. Every day I battle self-control. When I don't fight this battle against myself, I'm the one who suffers. If I let myself get out of control, I mentally berate myself. Instead, I'm learning to discipline my temper and my words. It's getting easier all the time.

Today's Tip: When you and your loved one leave the house, always take a sweater or jacket for her — especially in the evening or when going to a restaurant.

OCTOBER 6

I wouldn't be human if I didn't grieve the gradual loss of the relationship my loved one and I have shared. It isn't practical to pretend it can remain the same under the present circumstances and inevitable changes. The relationship must adapt. I am open to the new relationship that is forming. I will do all I can to make it a good connection.

Today's Tip: If your loved one won't sit still long enough for a complete meal, consider handing him soft finger foods and sandwiches. He can eat and pace at the same time. Mashed potatoes hold sandwiches together better than slippery mayonnaise. Most liquids can be frozen into popsicles. Use your imagination!

OCTOBER 7

I watch out for my loved one's safety from outside forces. I am also called upon to protect her from herself. Her declining memory and judgment prevents her from discriminating between what is safe and unsafe. I must be on the alert for potential hazards and react with the same loving concern I would afford a small child.

Today's Tip: If you have potentially hot or dangerous appliances that can't be put out of sight, you might try printing some *STOP* signs in big bold letters and attaching them to the appliances.

OCTOBER 8

Caregiving is one of the many facets of my life. It is a very important part of me, but I must not entirely neglect the other aspects of my identity. I must wear more than one hat so that I can be the best caregiver possible and keep my spirit refreshed.

Today's Tip: Clothes with lots of pockets are great for people with dementia who hoard special possessions or worry about having items such as keys and wallets in a safe place. Pockets can provide a sense of security.

OCTOBER 9

Although I watch our finances carefully, I realize the value in affording some pleasures. Life has not come to a halt. I can pamper myself once in a while with a well-deserved luxury. I am worth it!

Today's Tip: Warm baths are relaxing. Bubble baths are luxurious. Whirlpools are soothing to tired muscles. You can make your bathtub into a whirlpool relatively inexpensively. Call your plumber or plumbing supply house. They can recommend the best way to convert your tub.

OCTOBER 10

Home is a place that can't always be defined. It seems to be more of an inward concept than an actual location. Feeling at home is a state of security. When my loved one asks to go home, I imagine he is searching for a security he has lost touch with. I must realize I can't find his home for him. What I can do is help to make his quality of life as secure and peaceful as I can. I must never feel guilty when he asks for home. He is in many ways searching for himself.

Today's Tip: You may want to remove mirrors if your loved one no longer recognizes his own image. He might be looking for the reflection of a much younger person.

OCTOBER 11

I am financially literate. Based on the present circumstances, I have sought out the advice of professionals as well as family members. I have made appropriate adjustments. I know the considerations and choices I have in planning for the future. Comprehending the facts helps me a great deal.

Today's Tip: Updating wills, getting accounts and credit in your name, and many other financial considerations are in order. Don't delay. Make sure you have good financial counsel and an attorney well versed in elder law.

OCTOBER 12

Not only is laughter a wonderful momentary release, I've discovered it has fairly long-lasting healing power. Laughter releases endorphins into our systems. Endorphins are the body's natural pain killers. They help alleviate both physical and emotional pain. I make sure my loved one and I take a few doses of laughter every day!

Today's Tip: If your loved one spoke another language in childhood, try playing music with words sung in her native language. It may delight her and be more familiar than English.

OCTOBER 13

I don't project the next problem. I take each moment as it comes. I am prepared without agonizing over what might happen next. I am as apt to experience something positive as I am something negative. I am in control of giving a positive response — whatever I experience.

Today's Tip: Strips of bright colored tape on the edges of stairs will help your loved one see the changes in elevation more clearly. Provide handrails on at least one side of the stairwell.

OCTOBER 14

When planning a trip, I consider my loved one. Would he relax, or could the change cause too many problems? Will he have fond memories, or will he forget the vacation as soon as it is over? I must weigh many factors. In the long run, I may be doing both of us a favor if I go by myself and obtain safe care for him while I take a break.

Today's Tip: If you are flying with your loved one, notify the airline and airport that you are traveling with a memory-impaired family member. They can provide any assistance you may need. Be sure you hold the tickets, luggage stubs, passports, or any important papers yourself. As always, make sure he has identification on him – including your flight numbers, destinations, and addresses of places you will be staying.

OCTOBER 15

My loved one's lack of short term memory often works to our advantage. I can re-direct his thoughts when need be. I realize I can practice some of the same re-direction of my thoughts. I often dwell on the mistakes I make. I can't seem to forget them. The only person remembering them is me. I'm working on trying to forget negative things and channel my thoughts into other more positive areas.

Today's Tip: If your loved one refuses milk on his cereal, try ice cream instead. Ice cream is more fun than milk anyway!

OCTOBER 16

My loved one's doctor and I are partners. In fact, I am the partner with the day-to-day knowledge of what goes on. He is the consultant. I keep him informed of changes and call him when necessary. We have a good working relationship.

Today's Tip: Encourage your loved one to put on her own shoes and socks. It provides excellent stretching exercise. Tube socks are a good idea. There are no heels to worry about!

OCTOBER 17

I don't ask my loved one questions that rely on his memory. If we talk about the past, it is conversation he initiates and enjoys reminiscing about. When old music, pictures, movies, or anything triggers memories for him we are both delighted. I do not however, allow him to be questioned, badgered, or in any way humiliated by his inability to remember something.

Today's Tip: Memories can be triggered by sights, sounds, taste, touch and scents.

OCTOBER 18

Sometimes I just have to guess what is going on in my loved one's mind. I consider his wishes whenever possible. But, it is impossible to know how much he understands and does not understand. I have to concern myself more with his safety, comfort, and dignity than with what he thinks. If he is pleased or if something displeases him, I will know.

Today's Tip: Walking around a craft show, boat show, or antique show could prove to be a pleasant outing. There should be lots to see and much to stimulate memories.

OCTOBER 19

God helps me cope. He gives me solutions and answers I don't always expect. He sends some coping methods to me through other caregivers. Some answers I find in books. At times he slows me down and gives me time to figure things out myself. Sometimes he just leads me to do what feels best in my heart and it works!

Today's Tip: Remove all bones and any inedible garnishes from your loved one's plate. Also be aware paper napkins and Styrofoam cups can be eaten by mistake.

OCTOBER 20

I realize I am in an extraordinarily demanding situation. I can get stressed out. I acknowledge when my body is giving off warning signs. Stress can exhibit itself in the form of headaches or back pains. I might get edgy and cross. I may even catch myself grinding my teeth. When these or other symptoms of stress occur, I must accept help and realistically set some limits on what I can and cannot do.

Today's Tip: Sometimes pets can blend into the color of floors. Try to discourage your pet from lying in walkways where your loved one could trip over it.

OCTOBER 21

Interaction with other people is extremely important. Once in a while someone in my support group will say something that has a profound effect on me. It may be a comment that changes my whole way of thinking about something. The person may never know his words made such an impact on me. God has a way of using other people to get his messages across. People need people.

Today's Tip: If your loved one wears a hearing aid, check the batteries frequently and make sure it is functioning properly.

OCTOBER 22

Tasty goodies and smells from the kitchen bring warm and soothing feelings. Both taste and aroma offer great forms of sensory stimulation. My loved one and I enjoy the coziness of freshly baked goods or a delicious smelling meal. My work in the kitchen is a labor of love. I communicate attention and concern by offering him his favorite foods.

Today's Tip: Small blocks of wood and pieces of sandpaper can provide an excellent activity. Sanding is a good repetitive action that keeps active hands busy.

OCTOBER 23

My loved one has always liked to be a part of things. She has been an active participant in life. She still shows a tendency to want to be in on everything. I encourage her in all our activities. I accept her companionship and her degree of interest and participation. It is important she feels comfortable and included at all times.

Today's Tip: Water-proof half-slips save embarrassment and protect nice dresses and skirts. They can be removed and replaced easily when changing incontinent protection. Look for them in specialty catalogs.

OCTOBER 24

I have many interests. I never stop learning. My inquisitiveness keeps me going. I am never bored. Every experience offers something new for me. Every day I am challenged to increase my knowledge and awareness of the world around me.

Today's Tip: Public libraries offer many sources of free entertainment and education. Don't neglect to use this wonderful resource. Besides books and music, videos on numerous subjects are available. If transportation is a problem for you, most libraries offer shut-in services. Volunteers will deliver your selections right to your door!

OCTOBER 25

I have had to cultivate a gentleness I didn't possess in the past. I have become sensitive to the physical comfort as well as the emotional feelings of others. I try never to be rough. Gentleness is one of the many ways I communicate love in my caregiving.

Today's Tip: Often people with dementia like to fold things. One gentleman enjoyed folding tissues into tiny squares. Your loved one may like to fold the towels when they come out of the dryer.

OCTOBER 26

I need a place where I can ask questions and get straight-forward answers. I don't have time to fool around. At my support group, I get direct answers from people who have had the same questions and who experience the same eventful days I do. I have found a place where I get immediate help to cope with immediate problems.

Today's Tip: The use of public restrooms can present a problem if your loved one is a member of the opposite sex and relies on your assistance. Many caregivers carry an *Occupied* sign they hang on the door when they enter a restroom with their loved one. One caregiver carries an *Out of Order* sign. You'd be surprised how understanding and helpful strangers can be. Some will even offer to watch the door for you.

OCTOBER 27

I am committed to enjoying my loved one to the utmost. She cannot control the changes she is experiencing. I savor her current abilities. My closeness to her will enable me to help her as she continues to experience changes and as her abilities lessen. I cannot control the progression of the disease, but I can be an asset to my loved one.

Today's Tip: You may notice your loved one becoming less likely to initiate a conversation or suggest a new topic herself. When talking with her, let her know if you are changing the subject.

OCTOBER 28

I look forward to my support group meeting. I realize it is a safe place to release pent up tension. A feeling of trust and understanding permeates the air. We can share our feelings and fears openly. Both tears and laughter have filled our meeting room.

Today's Tip: If family is visiting from out of town, you might want to take them to a support group meeting with you. Visiting family members often attend with caregivers. A special bonding and strengthening can occur.

OCTOBER 29

I encourage my loved one's self-expression. When he seems pleased about something or initiates communication, I am delighted. I give him my full attention. I realize he may not have the ability to communicate the way he used to, but I am aware of his need to express himself in whatever ways he can. I let him know he is important.

Today's Tip: Building with a child's toy set can be a creative and fulfilling activity. Also children's workbenches with large plastic screws and bolts can prove interesting and enjoyable. Children's activities do not have to seem child-like if you present them in the right manner.

OCTOBER 30

When one person in a family is deeply affected by something, the whole family is affected. This is not a personal disease. It is a family disease. As the primary caregiver, I do not try to protect or hide the consequences of the disease from other family members.

Today's Tip: If some members of your family do not understand the effects of the disease because they only visit for an hour or two at a time, consider asking them to spell you for a day. They should get the picture and you'll get a day off!

OCTOBER 31

Keeping up a deception is exhausting and boring. Alzheimer's is a disease, not a crime. There is no need or advantage in denying its existence. I have enough to handle without worrying about covering up something that needs to be out in the open.

Today's Tip: Don't let your loved one ever feel she has done something wrong or that she is a burden. Include her in family decisions and conversations whenever you can.

NOVEMBER

NOVEMBER 1

I hurt for my loved one as I helplessly watch him struggle to make sense of things he no longer understands. His ability to search for and use clues seems to be slipping through his fingers. He seems unable to learn new information. I search for ways to ease his struggle. I cannot replace his losses, but I can help provide a peaceful and happy atmosphere for him every day.

Today's Tip: If communication is becoming increasingly difficult, try drawing, pointing to, or touching objects you are conversing about. Introduce these new ways of conversing in a matter-of-fact manner.

Sometimes my biggest problem is that my loved one doesn't realize she has a problem. She thinks I am a problem! My challenge is to keep her safe, clean, and well-fed without upsetting her. I don't want to create any undue stress for her. I must at the same time care for someone who doesn't seem to think she needs my care or my presence.

Today's Tip: Try to replace something you must remove with something new. For instance, if you have to take your loved one's credit cards away, she may be content with a different kind of plastic card that cannot be used for cash or purchases and presents no problem if lost.

NOVEMBER 3

It only takes a short time to make something a habit. There are good habits and there are bad habits. I had to make myself buckle my seat belt for about two months before it became a habit. I had to overcome my will to resist it. Now I don't even think about it — I buckle up before I start the engine! So it is with developing the good habit of asking for God's help every day. I begin each day by asking God for his help before I even get up and start my own engine. It's a great habit!

Today's Tip: An evening walk after dinner may help prevent night wandering.

Family bonding is important, especially when faced with the unusual and disturbing situations we AD families find ourselves in. Supporting one another is crucial. If I do not have the support I need from my family members, I must find support elsewhere. I may find a substitute family through the AD support group, neighbors, friends, or through my religious affiliation.

Today's Tip: Sometimes the need to touch is the greatest need of all.

NOVEMBER 5

My loved one's humor has become child-like. It is no longer brought out by understanding adult concepts or the adult subtleties of language. He laughs freely at cartoons and children's jokes. Joining him brings out the playful child in me. My inner child laughs with him. We laugh together from our hearts.

Today's Tip: Be aware that three-way conversations can be disturbing to your loved one. They are more difficult to follow than one-on-one conversations.

NOVEMBER 6

Among the changes my loved one and I
are experiencing is a change in our emotional
relationship. We don't fill all the same roles for
each other we once did. She depends on me for
support, while I am having to depend more on
others. We no longer relate on the same
emotional terms. I am learning to be more
independent. Part of this independence is
forming new connections and strengths.

Today's Tip: If your loved one needs help
dressing, slip each piece of clothing on with a
kiss. It may set the tone for the day.

NOVEMBER 7

My loved one can't try harder, while every day I feel I have to try harder. I get physically and mentally tired. I can't allow myself to cultivate thoughts of resentment. I also must not allow myself to get over-tired. I will work on cultivating the art of allowing others to help me cope. I need some regularly scheduled breaks from the constant demands of caregiving.

Today's Tip: If wandering outside is a problem, try removing objects from sight that might suggest going outdoors. These objects could be hats, jackets, purses, or even the dog's leash.

NOVEMBER 8

I am never given more than I can handle. But, I need to consider new ways of handling something if the old ways are no longer working for me. I am open to new ideas, new solutions, and new arrangements if they are called for.

Today's Tip: All decisions need to be based on what is realistically best for you and your loved one. Don't do something you really don't want to do because you feel you should or you think it is expected of you.

NOVEMBER 9

Life is not just today. It involves a much larger picture. I need to remember this fact to keep today and my place in it in the right perspective. Life is larger than me or any one day. I thank God for this realization today.

Today's Tip: Young children may surprise you in their loving consideration of the family member with Alzheimer's. Children often see things more clearly and simply than adults. One family was enjoying a meal in a restaurant when their loved one became restless and wanted to leave between each course. His granddaughter was sitting next to him and every time he started to get up from the table, she quietly rubbed his arm and nestled up against him. This sensitive, non-verbal gesture calmed him down beautifully.

NOVEMBER 10

My loved one doesn't act rude or say inappropriate things intentionally. He has just forgotten how to act in some situations. I try to avoid situations that trigger such behavior. When caught off-guard, I react in a matter-of-fact manner and remain composed and in control.

Today's Tip: Inappropriate sexual behavior can be quite perplexing, dangerous, or embarrassing. It could be a return to adolescent or child-like behavior. The intent may not be sexual at all. Whatever the cause, if you experience this in your loved one, remember he may not even realize who you are. Your comfort level and safety are of utmost importance at all times. Don't be afraid to talk about this or any other behavior problem with a trained professional.

NOVEMBER 11

I'm attached to people, not things. I need to keep in touch with the people who are close to me. Lack of touch and not keeping in touch could be interpreted as a form of rejection. I value all the important people in my life. I will reach out and touch them today in whatever ways I can. Touch reinforces love and trust.

Today's Tip: Make sure your loved one's slacks or trousers are not too long. If there has been a weight loss, the length may have to be shortened to avoid the possibility of tripping.

NOVEMBER 12

I involve my neighbors and friends in my life. An extra hand and companionship are most appreciated when I am faced with difficult tasks or undertakings. There are times I need help getting my loved one to appointments or in and out of the car. Often I need another voice to encourage my loved one. Sometimes I just like the emotional support and backing another person can provide.

Today's Tip: Some edible materials make safe craft supplies. For instance, bread dough can be used for clay and yogurt can be used instead of paint.

NOVEMBER 13

On days when my loved one seems listless I don't force him to interact with a lot of people. On such days pep talks are useless. It's best to just relax and have a quiet reassuring day together. I can sit by his side, pat his hand, and use it as a day to put my feet up and take it easy myself!

Today's Tip: Sometimes you might just have to give your loved one a graceful way out of a stressful situation.

NOVEMBER 14

I've had to come to the realization my loved one doesn't always think of others like she used to. She is not always considerate of others. She is more concerned with her own inner world which seems to be getting smaller all the time. I don't know if this is caused by fear or by the damage her brain is experiencing. All I know is her world doesn't always seem to include us. I am thankful for the occasional moments when our worlds interact.

Today's Tip: When constipation is a problem for your loved one, try a stool softener rather than a laxative. Talk to your doctor or pharmacist. Stool softeners can be purchased at the drug store in liquid or pill form.

NOVEMBER 15

I try to treat every situation my loved one and I encounter as perfectly normal. I believe I am helping preserve his dignity by doing so. I also keep my stress level more manageable by practicing an air of calmness and normalcy.

Today's Tip: Put a rubber sheet over the mattress if your loved one experiences incontinence during the night. Large disposable absorbent sheets to lay under him are available also. Smaller ones are made for chair seats.

NOVEMBER 16

I try not to take what my loved one says and does personally. She recognizes fewer people all the time. I am not surprised when the only ones she can attack, blame, or suspect are those of us who remain closest to her. It's easier when I remind myself of the fact she does not do things to me on purpose. She is angry at her situation — not at me. I can be angry at the situation, too, but I can control my anger and not add to her distress by directing my anger at her.

Today's Tip: A bean bag toss can be a safe enjoyable way to exercise muscles and help retain coordination.

NOVEMBER 17

I have to make many decisions for my loved one. I am constantly making new ones based on his current level of ability. His abilities often vary from day to day. I encourage as much self-care as possible. His body and mind need the exercise. One of the decisions I made early-on was not to help him do anything he can safely do by himself!

Today's Tip: Old elementary school readers could be great sources of easy reading and memory stimulation. Try to know your loved one's current reading and comprehension level. Don't embarrass him by presenting something that is too easy. If you mistakenly do this, calmly explain you've made a mistake and the book must belong to someone else.

NOVEMBER 18

My loved one doesn't always interpret what she hears accurately. She is sensitive to most noises. Noises often confuse and startle her. I close windows and doors, turn down radios and television sets, and generally supervise all the noises around our home.

Today's Tip: It's not a good idea to talk to someone with dementia over a home intercom system. It could cause great confusion!

NOVEMBER 19

With the holiday season approaching, I remind myself that even though this is joyful time of the year, it can be filled with many emotions and may even present some problems. I will try to remember this fact early and be extra good to myself and my loved one. I will not put undue stress on either of us. I will not have expectations that cannot be met and I will not participate in tiring activities or overdone festivities to please other people.

Today's Tip: Keep your routine as normal as possible during the demanding holiday season. Make this decision now before you get caught in a holiday frenzy!

NOVEMBER 20

I don't give my loved one too much advanced warning for activities or out-of-the-ordinary social functions. He is more apt to fret than look forward to the event. I generally tell him about it one-half hour before we have to go. That is enough time to get ready. I meet less resistance this way and both of our lives are less stressful.

Today's Tip: Some caregivers have simplified cold weather outer clothing for their loved ones by sewing scarves onto coat collars. If hats are a problem, coats and jackets with attached hoods work well. Mittens can be easier than gloves.

NOVEMBER 21

Cabin fever can become a real problem especially during the winter season, even in the best of situations. My loved one may or may not experience it. I try to stay aware of what she is feeling. When we both need a change of scenery, I try to provide it. If she seems content and I need to get out more, I make the proper arrangements to do so.

Today's Tip: One caregiver took a four-day respite and went to the Rose Bowl Parade. She came home refreshed and had many beautiful pictures to enjoy. Another caregiver said he had his passport renewed — just for the fun of it!

NOVEMBER 22

This is a giving time of the year. I'm approaching giving with a somewhat new attitude. I must selfishly protect my loved one's and my energy and emotional levels. I have to give myself some slack and not overdo in the giving of my time and energy in order to keep providing quality care. Those who truly care and know us will understand.

Today's Tip: Try to keep gift-giving in the proper perspective. Give yourself the gift of shopping early. Try some new methods of shopping. Order from catalogs. Give magazine subscriptions. You can charge store gift certificates on your store credit card over the phone and they'll mail them to you or to the recipient.

NOVEMBER 23

I cannot please other people or meet their unrealistic demands on me without ultimately hurting myself and my relationships. If I do something I don't want to do just to please someone else, I will harbor unhealthy resentments. I must be honest and realistic with others and with myself.

Today's Tip: Changing or breaking some old traditions is not a sin. The results could prove delightful for all concerned.

NOVEMBER 24

When my loved one and I visit family or friends, I plan ahead. If his attention span has decreased, I bring small things that please him. I include discrete repetitive activities to keep him quietly busy. If he likes to watch football on television or take walks around the yard or neighborhood, I ask one of the family members or friends ahead of time if they will help in these areas. If he is restless, perhaps one of the men could take him for a short car ride. We can all help to make it a good time for everyone.

Today's Tip: Your loved one may wish to go home before you are ready to call it a day. His concept of time might not be what it used to be. Do what you normally do to redirect his thoughts or behavior — whatever usually works!

NOVEMBER 25

I keep my reactions to AD research breakthroughs in the proper perspective. I remain objective. I know I must be realistic about the level my loved one is in. I discuss current findings and their effect on us with our doctor and my AD support group. I pray daily for a cure and prevention of this debilitating disease. The future of so many is dependent upon continued quality research.

Today's Tip: Some people experiencing dementia repeatedly remove their clothes. Nice looking jumpsuits can be purchased or made for either men or women that zip up the back. This attire preserves dignity rather than putting someone's clothes on backwards.

NOVEMBER 26

I have to give to myself on a regular basis to be able to keep giving to others. It's kind of a natural flow. If I neglect my own needs, my empathy for the needs of others does not come easily. When I am content, it flows naturally.

Today's Tip: Don't skip your AD support group meetings or your primary source of support during the holidays. It's a gift you must give yourself!

NOVEMBER 27

I have not forgotten how to enjoy life! Good times, good friends, good food, good entertainment are all a part of living. I may not participate as often as I used to, but when I do, I allow myself to have a great time. I'm not a party-pooper!

Today's Tip: Many family caregivers refer to day care as the Club. Your loved one may enjoy being a member!

NOVEMBER 28

I am not a teacher. I am a helper. I help my loved one function at his current level. I do things with him. I aid him whenever he needs assistance. I help keep him safe, but I don't attempt to explain his safety to him. He wouldn't understand. What I hope he understands and remembers is that I love him. That's why I'm here with him.

Today's Tip: Your loved one may enjoy jigsaw puzzles that have large sturdy pieces.

Sometimes strangers offer help. They seem to sense the child-like qualities in my loved one. Perhaps they lend a hand because they see me struggle to help him up from a chair or into the car. Whatever the reason, I thank God for these kind gestures offered by people we don't know and who don't know us. God bless them!

Today's Tip: Some dementia patients may wander because they live in the past and are trying to go to former jobs or carry out old responsibilities. A door to the outside can be camouflaged with a curtain to discourage wandering. Some caregivers have had good results by removing doorknobs and placing locks at the bottom of doors near the floor.

NOVEMBER 30

There are times my house and my mind just need a good old-fashioned house cleaning. My thoughts as well as my ceilings need the cobwebs removed. My cupboards and my emotions need better organization. While my muscles stretch with the physical aspects of cleaning, my mind clears itself of unnecessary burdens and anxieties. A good spring housecleaning can be a boon any time of the year!

Today's Tip: If unwanted door-to-door sales people present disruptions and are a problem to you or your loved one, consider posting a sign near your front entrance prohibiting solicitations.

DECEMBER

DECEMBER 1

Although I try not to take any of my loved one's actions, behaviors, or comments personally, I must admit I do get hurt. I have a hard time getting used to the fact she doesn't always know who I am. At times she calls me by her brother's name. Perhaps it is because the dementia has brought her back to her childhood. If that is so, it should be no surprise to me when she can't remember my name or my birthday. She never means to hurt me.

Today's Tip: One gentleman with AD did not recognize his wife of many years by name, but he always told her he loved her and wanted to marry her. On their fiftieth wedding anniversary they renewed their marriage vows with close friends and family attending. It was a joyous occasion for everyone.

DECEMBER 2

I understand when my loved one chooses to be an observer, rather than a participant. At times he is content to watch things going on around him. He smiles and seems connected in a tranquil way. I don't push him when he appears to be enjoying the world around him.

Today's Tip: If you send greeting cards, your loved one may enjoy helping. Depending on his level of ability and his attention span, he may be able to help sign the cards, address them, put them in envelopes, seal the envelopes and affix the stamps. When you receive cards, read them together and then display them. The names of old friends may trigger memories and inspire pleasant conversation.

DECEMBER 3

My loved one needs the love and attention of other people in addition to what she gets from me. When I am busy with household chores or other projects she doesn't get much of my attention. Day care has helped a great deal. When she is there she is part of a social group. She interacts with others on her own, apart from me. I am pleased she has the opportunity for self-fulfillment and renewed self-esteem. She has formed her own social group there.

Today's Tip: You can purchase recordings of old radio programs for your loved one's enjoyment. She may want to take them to share with her friends at day care.

DECEMBER 4

I am redundant. I find myself repeating questions, answers, and directions. I feel like a nag. But I remind myself that when my repetitions are delivered in a loving manner, I am showing patience. Patience cannot be mistaken for nagging. I offer repeated words and reassurances with compassion. I am not a nag.

Today's Tip: Pants and trousers with drawstring waists are very comfortable and allow for changes in weight. Wrap-around skirts are excellent for the ladies!

DECEMBER 5

Decorating the house for the holidays generally brings a positive, joyful response. Old familiar decorations can bring back fond memories. My loved one and I enjoy making garlands, baking cookies, and listening to holiday music together.

Today's Tip: Caregivers sometimes wisely replace breakable holiday decorations with ones made of Styrofoam, wood, or fabric. Be extra careful to ensure safety and don't change furniture around to accommodate holiday decorations. Be aware that poinsettias and mistletoe can be quite harmful if ingested.

DECEMBER 6

Music has always had a special meaning for my loved one and me. We still enjoy attending musical programs together – especially this time of the year. Family sing-a-longs to favorite carols have become an activity my loved one joyfully joins.

Today's Tip: Recorded Christmas music is available at no charge through the public library. Also, radio stations play a great deal of it during the holidays. Christmas movie classics can be rented at video stores or purchased at most discount stores. Watching them together may be a relaxing holiday activity.

DECEMBER 7

There are many reasons for thankfulness. When faced with the burdens of life it is good to pause and mentally count blessings. Sometimes I even sit and write them down one by one. It proves to be a positive exercise. I come out of it a happier, more content person. I give thanks to God today for the many blessings he has bestowed upon me.

Today's Tip: Put your loved one's ID bracelet on the wrist of his dominant hand. It will be more difficult for him to remove.

DECEMBER 8

I am only restrictive in matters concerning my loved one's safety or her overall well-being. For the most part, I encourage her self-expression and independence. I watch that she does not get over-tired or over-stressed. Her state of well-being is a major concern of mine at all times.

Today's Tip: When you safety check the house, check the garage too. Depending on your loved one's level of dementia you may want to lock up things like saws, hedge clippers, and insecticides.

DECEMBER 9

I don't expect to do the impossible. I can't accomplish all the things I used to before I added caregiving to my life. I must be especially aware of this during the holiday season. I have to be as considerate of myself and my limitations as I am of my loved one's. We are both under more stress, tire more easily, and require more TLC than under normal conditions.

Today's Tip: Many caregivers keep a list of activities handy for days when their loved ones are unusually restless or exhibit short attention spans. If your loved one likes to rummage through drawers or your things, make him a rummaging box of his own. It might keep his attention for quite a while.

DECEMBER 10

Sometimes I doubt myself. Am I doing things right? Am I doing the right things? I know there are no rights or wrongs when it comes to caregiving. I must basically go with my instincts. I do know right from wrong in the context of relationships with others and how I relate to them. I know gentleness is always better than roughness. I find peace knowing I treat others with the kindness I would want from them were I in the same situation.

Today's Tip: Hide a spare house key somewhere outside the house. Many AD loved ones accidentally lock their family caregivers out.

DECEMBER 11

I recognize the needs of others. I recognize my needs also. There is no reason for comparison or definition of urgency. Our needs are equally important. Fairness puts us on an equal plane. The balance makes sense and makes life more natural for all of us.

Today's Tip: Baking cookies is a fun part of the holidays. Involve your loved one in mixing, rolling, cutting out, sprinkling — and, of course, sampling!

DECEMBER 12

I used to take things for granted. Now I appreciate each and every moment of pleasure. I find enjoyment in smaller things. I recognize pleasant occurrences. I take time and relish things I may have overlooked in the past. A smile, laughter, a coherent comment, an acknowledgment, all warm my heart and I enjoy them. They are no longer taken for granted.

Today's Tip: Gift certificates to favorite restaurants are fun to give and to receive!

DECEMBER 13

My journal gives me insight into my thoughts and helps me with caregiving. It could also prove to be a valuable resource if something were to happen to me and someone else had to continue in my caregiving role. It is full of important data for day-to-day caregiving and understanding of my loved one and our situation. Keeping a journal is just another caring thing I do!

Today's Tip: Keep a current list of emergency and important telephone numbers handy. In an emergency a phone book can be extremely difficult to use.

DECEMBER 14

Physical exercise is an easy way to reduce stress. Somehow it sets up a cycle of feeling good all over. It does wonders for me mentally as well as physically. I make sure I do some regular exercising on my own. My abilities and needs are not the same as my loved one's. I take time to have a sensible exercise routine or engage in a favorite sport for myself. It's a great habit and promotes my good health.

Today's Tip: Many AD patients enjoy cutting things out. Simple decorations can be made from Christmas cards. Cutting coupons out of the newspaper is a helpful activity. Don't forget to keep a couple of pairs of blunt scissors on hand!

DECEMBER 15

I have confidence in myself. I trust my instincts. I have a sense of accomplishment when I help my loved one enjoy his day. I know I can't offer him a cure, but I can offer him my love and support. I don't put unrealistic expectations on either one of us. We're both doing the best we can one day at a time.

Today's Tip: If your loved one starts a project and doesn't finish it, don't make a big deal out of it. If he gets upset with himself, try to distract him with something pleasant. Go back and quietly finish the project yourself when it's convenient for you.

DECEMBER 16

I try to avoid activities that don't cheer me. This is a season of good cheer and I choose to do the things I enjoy. I don't involve myself in things I know will be hard for me or my loved one. I am clear about this to my family and friends. We adapt activities to what we can handle physically and emotionally. Necessary changes in holiday traditions can be positive. This isn't a time for comparisons. It's a time for peace and goodwill.

Today's Tip: Treat yourself to the holiday things you find heartwarming. Get out and see the lights. Attend a holiday style show or concert. Help someone who is less fortunate than you.

DECEMBER 17

I've learned to substitute old ways of doing things with new ways. I use my common sense and my ingenuity. If an old way becomes too difficult, frustrating, or time consuming, I replace it with a new and better way for now. I recognize when a change is necessary and appropriate.

Today's Tip: Early day celebrations may be more appropriate than evening festivities. Small gatherings can be more peaceful than large groups. Buffet dinners with many food choices and plate balancing might be too confusing and frustrating for your loved one. You know best what can be handled comfortably.

DECEMBER 18

Making choices is good for all of us. It helps give us a sense of personal control. I realize too many choices can be confusing for my loved one. Being able to make a few choices is good for her. Whenever the opportunity arises to be able to safely offer her choices, I am happy to do so.

Today's Tip: If you can, involve your loved one in gift selections. She may be interested in making small choices between two items or in choosing gift wrapping. When she receives gifts, help her unwrap them if she needs help. Explain the gifts and demonstrate how to use them.

DECEMBER 19

There are some people who just seem to brighten the lives of those around them — just by their presence. Their smiles are contagious. Their outlook on life is contagious. They are always uplifting. I seek out those people in my life. What a blessing they are!

Today's Tip: Be good to yourself. The holidays can be a hard time when you are involved in caregiving. Surround yourself with good thoughts. Spend quality time with positive friends and family members. Reach out to others.

DECEMBER 20

I arrange and make plans that fit best for me and my loved one. Medical appointments are appropriately scheduled to coincide with our least stressful daytime periods. I always accompany my loved one the whole time. I can help him cooperate and communicate. I don't have to rely on his memory of what was said and done or take more of the doctor's time than is necessary.

Today's Tip: Some caregivers write down their questions, concerns, or observations before seeing the doctor. They discretely give them to the nurse or receptionist when they arrive for the appointment.

DECEMBER 21

My loved one and I are fascinated by a kaleidoscope. The bright colored shapes and pieces are constantly changing. It reminds me of life and its many changes. Each pattern, each sequence is unique. We spend some time with it and then it is gone. We can't ever get it back exactly the same way it was. We better enjoy it while we have it and not try to get it back. We must go on to the next combination of brightly colored fragments and reflections. They are all special and should be enjoyed.

Today's Tip: Drinking a glass of cranberry juice every day can help reduce the risk of urinary infections. Use pure cranberry juice — not a mixture of juices or flavors.

DECEMBER 22

My time is mine. It doesn't make any difference what time of the year it is. If I choose to do something novel with my time, the decision is mine. If I choose to do something special or not to do anything special with my time, the decision is mine. I do know that I am special and what I do every day in caregiving is very special. I rejoice in that knowledge and in the simple pleasures of each season.

Today's Tip: Your loved one may experience a decrease or loss in her sense of smell. She might not be able to tell if food has spoiled. Don't keep leftovers in the refrigerator too long!

DECEMBER 23

I feel secure knowing I am a child of God. It doesn't matter what age I am. I have a loving father who cares for me. He guides me and helps me through difficult times. I give him praise and thanks. I get joy and strength from him.

Today's Tip: Crowds and crowded spaces may bother your loved one. She needs space to move. If she attends a large social gathering be aware of this and seek out a quiet space large enough for her to feel comfortable and able to function in.

DECEMBER 24

I am thankful for the true meaning and significance of the holidays. My faith is a big part of my life. It gives me strength and confidence. I am never alone. I celebrate the joy of the season in my heart. I know the true meaning of love.

Today's Tip: Reading of the scriptures, prayers, and worshipping may all still have special meaning to your loved one. Don't refrain from sharing special spiritual times and activities with him.

DECEMBER 25

I pray a Christmas prayer. I am filled with awe. I am struck with the simplicity of the redeeming Christmas message. A child came for the whole world. God sent peace and forgiveness to mankind. His love glowed in a child's heart. God's message came through his words. Christmas need not be just this day. God offers us his perfect gift every day of the year. All we have to do is accept his gift. We'll still go through both the joys and pains of life, but his peace and love can fill us and glow in our hearts, too.

Today's Tip: The Christmas message doesn't change — Merry Christmas! Peace and love to you and yours. Pass this peace — it's meant to be shared!

DECEMBER 26

My days may not always run smoothly. They may be filled with some changes in behaviors and plans. Still there is a blanket of comfort in the routine we have developed. Through problems I have found a workable level of operation. By trial and error I have discovered which tools of coping work best for me. I can enjoy the blessings of daily living. My coping skills are among them.

Today's Tip: It's best not to tell your loved one you pay for day care or in-home help. Many AD loved ones respond well to the idea of being volunteers. They feel they are helping others at the day care facility.

DECEMBER 27

I try to find the reason for a behavior problem. It is better for me to find the cause and deal with it than to over react to the problem. The way I react is to distract, dissuade, or redirect my loved one. At times I ignore the problem — whatever works immediately. Then I go back and think through what happened just prior to the difficult behavior. Is it a recurrent behavior? Often I find clues that uncover the reasons.

Today's Tip: People can become restless for any number of reasons. You may not be able to determine why your loved one is restless, but you might be able to provide her with a comforting distraction by taking her for a walk or a car ride.

DECEMBER 28

I rejoice in the simple pleasures around me. My heart is warmed by them. I see beauty in the unadorned. I love the purity of nature — the clean simplicity of natural things. Grace and charm abound in homespun treasures. My surroundings are comfortable and peaceful. I am content. Indeed, I am wealthy — not rich.

Today's Tip: If your loved one gets lost, he may not admit or realize he is lost. He may fear you are lost and won't be able to find him. When you are reunited, don't argue over who was lost.

DECEMBER 29

I am trustworthy. Others can trust me. When a friend has a problem or something he needs to talk through, I listen. I don't share what I have heard with anyone else. What my friend tells me stays with me. I can be counted on. I am a good friend. Conversely, when I need someone to talk to I seek out a trusted friend. I am fortunate to have someone I can confide in.

Today's Tip: If your loved one experiences choking at meals, have his doctor examine him to make sure there is no physical problem in his throat. If the doctor finds it is strictly a dementia issue, ask him if serving solid foods with the consistency of applesauce or pudding will help. He may provide you with a list of foods he considers safe. He may also suggest some liquids be thickened with a commercial thickener or to try liquids such as eggnog and apricot juice.

DECEMBER 30

The children and teens in our family are an important part of the family unit. They are involved in the concerns of the family. They help when they can. However, they are not grown-ups and we do not saddle them with adult responsibilities. To do so would not be fair to them or anyone.

Today's Tip: Teens sometimes insulate themselves. They can appear not to care when they care deeply. Offering to help with anything, let alone caregiving, is a lot to expect. They may be embarrassed by some behavior changes in the AD family member. Young children need to be reassured they are not the cause of any of the loved one's behavior changes or the stress the family might be experiencing. Encourage the children and teens in your family to talk about their feelings with someone they trust. Teens in particular might feel more comfortable talking with someone outside the family unit.

DECEMBER 31

This has been a year full of changes. Along with the changes, I have changed. I have grown. I have achieved things I never knew I was capable of. I am more patient. I am more kind. I am more understanding. I still have work to do. There will be more changes. I will continue to make informed decisions and use the tools I have been given. Along with reaching within to my inner resources I will continue to reach out to others and to my God. We are a team!

Today's Tip: Don't forget, caregiving is an awesome responsibility and you're not expected to do it alone!

About the poem for the family caregiver . . .

I have been touched by the many poems, prayers, and personal experiences submitted to the Alzheimer's Association chapter newsletters around the country. One poem in particular spoke to my heart. It was written by Janet Angela Romans, formerly Janet Jensen, and published in the Fall 1991 issue of the Southeastern Wisconsin Chapter newsletter. In July, 1995 I called the chapter hoping to be able to locate the author of the poem and obtain her permission to use the poem in the opening of this book. To my delight, she was right there in the chapter office and I was able to speak to her immediately! We became instant friends as do most people who share a family experience with Alzheimer's. I am looking forward to meeting Janet in person soon. She has written a number of poems and prayers for her chapter newsletters and I hope she will continue sharing and blessing others through this beautiful gift of hers.

L.R.

A POEM FOR THE FAMILY CAREGIVER

by Janet Angela Romans

It all seemed to start so slowly, subtle things so easily missed,
A forgotten name, repeated words, or lips no longer kissed;
'Till one day you knew that something was, indeed, cause for alarm,
And you took the steps so needed, to protect and save from harm;

Many moments you have witnessed changes you cannot control,
You couldn't know you'd find yourself, in this often thankless role;
But you brace yourself while tackling jobs you never thought you'd do,
As you shake your head in wonder, asking, "How AM I getting through?"

For awhile perhaps you hoped it was an ill that could be fixed,
Your emotions like a roller coaster, high and low . . . and mixed;
Then you learned that it was Alzheimer's and how, you too must change,
As you face dramatic happenings in your vast caregiving range;

With each day you square your shoulders as you lovingly dig in,
To the mountainous job before you, sadly knowing it's, "no win",
But because of love that's stronger than the hardest gem from coal,
You have chosen to find inner strength, on loan within your soul;

There'll come the day when you'll look back with feelings of great pride,
For the choice you've made to caringly stay at your loved one's side,
And God will bless your times of care, with memories He'll impart,
His gift of lifelong peace to live forever in your heart.

Index

A

ABILITIES: 2/21,7/28
ACCEPTANCE: 1/2,1/22,2/9,2/10,2/21,3/31,5/27,6/24,
9/3,9/18,10/31,
ACTION: 6/13
ACTIVITIES: 1/1,1/14,1/18,3/9,3/16,3/20,4/3,4/19,
5/9,5/10, 6/18,7/1,7/4,7/15,7/22,7/23,7/26,8/10,
8/29,8/30, 9/26,10/18,10/22,10/23,11/28,12/2,
12/5, 12/6,12/11,12/9,12/14
AFFECTION: 3/28
AFFIRMATION: 5/18,8/22,9/23,10/3
ANGER: 7/7,9/26,11/16
ANIMALS: 2/15,4/29,9/8,10/20
ATTITUDE: 1/11,2/1,2/4,2/5,3/9,3/25,4/14,4/16,
5/11,5/31,6/30,7/1,7/19,10/13,11/22
AUTHORITY: 1/26,5/23,9/22
AWARENESS: 1/30,7/2

B

BALANCE: 2/16,4/12,5/22,7/13,8/9,8/27,12/11
BATHING: 1/13,2/3,3/13,3/18,8/3,9/15,9/17,
9/20,10/9
BEHAVIOR: 3/6,4/2,4/9,4/25,8/3,8/15,8/24,10/5,11/10,
12/1,12/27
BLESSINGS: 1/20,6/30,11/29,12/7,12/12

BODY LANGUAGE: 3/14,3/24,8/2
BODY TEMPERATURE: 1/17,9/24,10/5

C

CALLING CARDS: 4/10,7/30
CHAIRS: 3/30,5/5,8/5,9/15
CHALLENGES: 2/5,4/11,7/7,11/2
CHANGE: 1/18,2/5,4/5,5/1,5/7,5/24,6/3,6/23,8/15,
8/20,9/7,10/27,11/6,12/17,12/21, 12/31
CHOICES: 2/8,2/20,3/4,5/25,8/8,9/16,12/16,12/18
CLOTHING: 6/16,6/17,6/29,10/5,10/8,11/11,11/20,
11/25,12/4
COMMON SENSE: 1/21,8/13,9/19
COMMUNICATION: 1/3,1/8,2/1,3/3,3/7,3/8,4/1,
4/12,5/18, 5/30,6/15,6/19,6/20,6/23,7/6,7/20,
7/23,7/28/11,8/27,9/7, 9/18,9/29,10/2,10/27,11/1,
8/11,8/27,9/7,9/18,9/29,10/2,10/27,11/1
COMPARISIONS: 3/3
COMPASSION: 3/12,5/24,7/2,7/21,9/17,9/22,9/24,
9/29,10/2,10/18,10/25,11/1,11/2,11/13,11/29,12/2
COMPLIMENTS: 3/27
COMPOSURE: 6/14,8/17,11/15
COMPREHENSION: 5/30,10/18
COMPROMISE: 7/13
CONFUSION: 7/14,7/16,7/18,7/29,8/4,8/17,8/30,
10/10,11/5,11/18
CONSISTENCY: 3/5,9/6
CONSTIPATION: 11/14
COOPERATION: 6/5,8/13,10/3
COPING: 2/10,7/8,10/19,11/7,12/26

F

FAITH: 2/2,6/12,7/29,8/1,12/23,12/24,12/25
FAMILY: 1/9,1/19,3/19,3/22,4/21,5/21,6/15,9/3,
9/9,9/29,10/28,10/30,11/4,11/9,12/30
FATIGUE: 2/4,2/23,4/7,5/7,5/9,6/28,7/4
FEAR: 2/2,3/23,5/2,8/21
FEELINGS: 4/8,5/12,6/20,8/3,9/29,10/22
FINANCES: 3/10,4/13,6/2,7/23,10/9,10/11,11/2
FLEXIBILITY: 2/14,6/2,8/4,9/20
FOCUS: 1/16,7/18
FORGIVENESS: 5/10
FREEDOM: 5/20,5/29
FRIENDS: 1/9,3/19,4/24,5/8,6/15,9/30

G

GADGETS: 4/26
GARDENING: 5/16
GIFTS: 5/1,6/21,11/22,11/26,12/12,12/18
GRIEF: 8/19,10/6
GROWTH: 5/15,12/31
GUILT: 1/6,4/22,5/23,6/16,7/7,10/10,11/8

H

HALLUCINATIONS: 5/19,7/5
HANDYMAN: 1/30
HAPPINESS: 3/2
HIDING THINGS: 1/28,3/1,8/8,9/19,10/8
HONESTY: 6/25,10/31

P

PACING: 5/11,8/5
PAIN: 3/10,4/30,7/14,9/24
PATIENCE: 1/20,2/25,7/25,8/5,12/4
PEACE: 4/28,5/12,5/21,6/3,6/14,7/5,8/4,8/15,9/22
PERFECTION: 3/26
PERSPECTIVE: 2/26,5/22,11/9,11/22
PHYSICAL STRENGTH: 1/16
PHYSICIAN: 4/4,7/12,10/16,12/20
PICTURES: 1/10,2/12,3/11,8/21
PRAISE: 2/7,3/12,9/23
PRAYER: 3/1,5/21,6/21,12/25
PRIORITIES: 1/11,11/3
PRIVATE TIME: 4/26,11/30

Q

QUIET TIME: 1/31,3/29

R

READING: 2/17,3/11,11/17,12/2
REALITY: 2/12,2/13,5/12,5/19,6/17,7/8,7/12,10/30,
10/31,11/14
REASONING: 1/21
REGRETS: 6/11
RELATIONSHIPS: 3/29,4/21,10/6,11/6,11/23
REPETITION: 5/25,5/26
RESENTMENT: 3/21,6/5,11/7,11/23
RESISTANCE: 3/15,7/11,8/23,9/11

RESOURCES: 1/4,1/19,5/4,7/28,9/3,9/5,10/24,10/26
RESPITE: 1/9,1/27,2/23,2/25,6/13,7/27,8/18,8/28,
9/8,9/10,10/14,11/21
REST: 5/28,7/4,11/13
RISKS: 3/30,8/14
ROLES: 3/22
RUMMAGING: 12/9

S

SAFETY: 2/6,2/20,3/27,4/11,4/30,5/21,6/4,6/7,
6/28,7/13,8/6,8/23,8/31,9/1,9/2,9/10,9/11,9/14,9/25,9/28,
9/29, 10/1,10/7,10/13,10/19,10/20,10/21,11/10,11/11,
11/12,12/5,12/7,12/8,12/10, 12/22,12/29
SCHEDULES: 3/4,6/10
SECRETS: 5/16
SELF-ACCEPTANCE: 2/15,7/5,10/29,12/9
SELF-AFFIRMATION: 7/30,8/12,10/24,12/10,12/15,
12/22,12/31
SELF-CONFIDENCE: 7/16,10/8
SELF-ESTEEM: 1/7,1/13,3/11,3/13,4/9,4/17,5/13,6/8,7/3
SELF-LOVE: 1/25,8/16
SENSITIVITY: 1/3,2/24
SERENITY: 1/6,2/20,3/26,6/3,6/19,9/2,12/28
SHADOWING: 3/2,9/12
SHARING: 1/24,2/18,6/13,6/27,8/2,8/18
SHOES: 3/27
SHOPPING: 1/25,4/23
SHOWERING: 1/13,2/18,2/22,4/2
SIGNS: 3/25,6/10,8/22,10/7,10/26
SKIN CARE: 3/18,9/10

SLEEP: 8/10,8/17,9/12,9/23
SMILES: 2/10
SOCIAL OCCASIONS: 4/6,8/1,11/20,11/24,11/27,
12/17,12/23
SOCIAL SKILLS: 1/23,4/6
SONGS: 4/27
SORTING: 2/13
STRENGTH: 4/3,9/15
STRESS:1/5,1/9,4/8,4/18,7/17,9/5,9/21,11/19,
11/20,12/14
SUCCESS: 1/29,6/4,6/8
SUNDOWNING: 5/4,6/11,8/14
SUPPORT: 1/4,2/24,4/20,4/24,5/1,5/3,5/6,5/8,
5/13, 6/9,6/27, 9/1,9/16,9/21,9/30, 10/21,10/26,
10/28,11/4, 11/12,11/26,12/19,
SURRENDER: 1/26

T

TEARS: 3/5,10/28
TELEPHONE: 4/28,9/5
TELEVISION: 1/29,2/19,5/12,10/4
TENSION: 3/15,7/4,10/28
TIMING: 9/19
TOUCH: 1/3,6/22,8/29,9/23,11/4,11/11
TOYS: 3/21,8/26,9/27,10/29
TRADITIONS: 5/17,6/26
TRANSPORTATION: 1/22,6/4,6/14,10/14
TRUST: 3/6,4/19,7/6,7/20,11/11,12/29

V

W

The author, Lyn Roche,
can be contacted by calling
800-596-2455.

Appendix 1

OTHER RESOURCES FROM ELDER BOOKS

Sharing The Care by Lyn Roche
This book addresses the many adjustments family members face when a loved one becomes a nursing home resident. **Sharing The Care** is written not only for family members of Alzheimer's patients, but for anyone who has a loved one living in a nursing home, assisted living center or congregate living facility. $11.95

Surviving Alzheimer's: A Guide For Families by Florian Raymond
Easily digestible, this book is a treasure house of practical tips, ideas and survival strategies for the busy caregiver. It describes how to renew and restore yourself during the ups and downs of caregiving, and shows you how to take care of yourself as well as your family member. $10.95

Show Me The Way To Go Home: by Larry Rose
Larry Rose was a vital, gifted engineer in his forties when Alzheimer's struck. In this first-person account, Rose shares his heartbreaking skirmishes with a disease he has been battling since its diagnosis in 1992. **Show Me The Way To Go Home** is a highly individual personal experience with universal appeal. $10.95

Gone Without A Trace by Marianne Caldwell
Stella Dickerman, an accomplished artist and weaver, vanished mysteriously on September 13th, 1991, two years after the onset of Alzheimer's disease. **Gone Without A Trace** is the gripping personal story of her daughter's quest for answers during the long search odyssey which ensued. $10.95

Failure-Free Activities For The Alzheimer's Patient by Carmel Sheridan
This award-winning book describes hundreds of simple, non-threatening activies which are suitable for persons with Alzheimer's disease. The author describes how to focus on the abilities that remain rather than the patient's deficits and to create activities which capitalize on existing strengths. $10.95

ORDER FORM

To: Elder Books
PO Box 490
Forest Knolls, CA 94933
PH: 1 800 909-COPE (2673) FAX: 415 488-4720

Please send me:

__ Copies of Coping With Caring   @ $11.95

__ Copies of Sharing The Care   @ $11.95

__ Copies of Surviving Alzheimer's   @ $10.95

__ Copies of Show Me The Way To Go Home   @ $10.95

__ Copies of Gone Without A Trace   @ $10.95

__ Copies of Failure-Free Activities   @ $10.95

SHIPPING: $2.75 For first book. $1.75 for each additional
book. CA residents, please add 8.25% sales tax.

Name: _____

Address: _____

City: _____

State: _____   Zip: _____

Amount enclosed: _____

__ CHECK HERE FOR FREE CATALOG